Psychological Keys to Student Success

Troy Dvorak

ISBN: 1505607930
ISBN-13: 978-1505607932

DEDICATION

<u>Mom</u>

The confidence I have, the goals I set, and the ends I achieve all stem from the unwavering, ubiquitous love and support you have given me. The example of love you set is one of the cornerstones of my career choices and desire to help others. I love you more than I can ever express.

<u>Big Sister</u>

The learning books you made me when I was a kid paid off! From the time I was little, you helped me value learning, become a good student, and (hopefully) become a good teacher. Baby Brother loves his Big Sister.

CONTENTS

ACKNOWLEDGMENTS

To my friends and colleagues who generously took the time to offer feedback about my early drafts of this book, I offer heartfelt gratitude. I am certain your input made it a ton better. However, if it does not sell well because people think it sucks, it's obviously your fault! **LOL**

So that no one can actually find you to blame you, I will only list your first names:

Miles	You are at the top of the blame list, buddy!
Elaine	You are sooo smart! Thanks for the great suggestions.
Doug	We've never even met face-to-face. But you're Elaine's hubby so you must be a good egg.
Leigh	I think you might be a closet rocker so you are ok in my book. No, not this book. Oh, you know what I mean. ☺
Dennis	You are a Scrabble geek. Why didn't you make more vocabulary suggestions? This book could have been a BINGO!
Jessica	Your suggestions were great. Wanna co-author something with me in the future?

INTRODUCTION TO THE PSYCHOLOGICAL KEYS TO STUDENT SUCCESS (PK2SS):

Teachers offer students advice on how to study all the time. You know what I'm talking about, right? They tell you about studying skills such as making flashcards, highlighting things you read, re-reading and memorizing, summarizing, and doing practice questions. But if you want to maximize your learning, you also need many <u>thinking skills</u>. You will read about both in this book, with a strong emphasis on teaching you **HOW TO THINK**. Thinking skills are NOT the same as studying skills. As you will see, THINKING skills will make your studying skills more effective. They will allow you to thrive, not just survive in college.

If you are like most college students, you have a lot to do. If you are straight out of high school and are taking a full course load, that is a lot to do all by itself. Many college students are "nontraditional" which means they may live independently from their parents, have a job (or jobs), have children, and/or be returning to school after taking a break. That means time is a precious commodity. So let's get right to it.

Consider this quotation: "Learning how to learn cannot be left to students. It must be taught."[1] Most people think about learning information when they go to college. They don't automatically think about learning how to learn. If you did well in high school, or if you are an adult coming to college after having some success in the work world, you probably don't think you need to learn how to learn. Some of you may be right.

Before you jump to that conclusion, there is another quotation I would like you to consider: "Seventy-nine percent of entering students at a community college reported that they felt either well prepared or adequately prepared for college-level work. However, after 2 years, 59% had left without earning a degree."[2] I know that sounds bad, but do not feel discouraged. In fact, you can feel hopeful (you'll just have to take my word for that at the moment). I wrote this book because I know that the **Psychological Keys to Student Success (PK2SS)** address the thinking skills and personal characteristics you can develop in order to succeed in college. For example, research reveals that having high academic goals, motivation, confidence in your own abilities, and self-control contribute to college retention and graduation.[3,4,5] Those aren't studying skills. They are thinking and personal skills.

It would be misleading, however, if I told you that hard work and good thinking skills will get all of you through to graduation. In psychology we know there are many factors related to academic achievement, including intelligence (that is a huge topic and is not the focus of this book).[6] A very smart colleague of mine offered a nice metaphor and I hope it will be helpful to you. Each one of us is like a rubber band when it comes to intelligence. We come in different sizes. There is nothing we can do to change the size of the rubber band we happen to be. However, we are all capable of stretching a lot! This book is all about the factors that will allow you to...

S - T - R - E - T - C - H !

So, what are your thoughts about how to be a successful college student? Is success in college about your intelligence? Getting good grades? Just passing? Memorizing? Learning?

Getting a degree? What exactly does a successful college student look like? Would you know a successful college student if you saw one? Is that person staring back at you in the mirror?

"Academic-intellectual work is heavily cognitive, requiring combinations of knowledge and reasoning skills."[7] What does that mean? I'm glad you asked because I'm going to tell you! It means that earning a college degree is hard work. It requires a lot of effort, some serious concentration, and a stick-with-it attitude. You need to develop many skills in order to keep up with the rigors of a college education. The first year of college is a pivotal time, where you will develop attitudes and approaches toward learning as well as your perception of yourself as a college student.[8]

Why did I write this book?

1. I'm a (cool) geek. When I'm not drumming and totally rockin' out, I love to review research in psychology. I love to learn. ☺
2. Decades of research show there are consistent differences between students who do well in college and those who do not. I have observed these differences personally as a teacher. I want you to know these differences.
3. Research articles contain a lot of good information but they are written in a way that is hard to understand. I want the information to be useful to you!
4. Combining my previous counseling experience with my current teaching experience, I have identified <u>ways people think</u> that are helpful and ways that are counterproductive.

5. Helping others is something I'm passionate about. I believe that sharing some of the research and my experience will help you.

My Goals for the Book:

1. **Teach you HOW TO THINK.**
2. Show you the difference between "studying skills" and "thinking skills" and convince you that you need BOTH, especially thinking skills.
3. Teach you psychological principles that will help you succeed in school and life.
4. Share research findings in a way you will find understandable and useful.
5. **Give you the keys to unlock student success!**

THE PSYCHOLOGICAL KEYS TO STUDENT SUCCESS (PK2SS)

Each Psychological Key to Student Success is a thinking skill or personal characteristic that can greatly improve your academic achievement and chances for college success. Don't worry about the fancy terms. By the time you are done reading this book, you will understand them all!

1. **Beliefs and Mindset**
2. **Attributions**
3. **Achievement Goals & Interest**
4. **Self-efficacy**
5. **Metacognition**
6. **Self-regulated Learning (SRL)**
7. **Thinking Errors**
8. **Culture**

Throughout the book you will see little numbers after many of the sentences. These refer to the notes section at the end of the book. That is where I provide references to the research I read and used to write this book. By doing that, other academic geeks like me can see that I did not just make this stuff up! I used about 200 references in writing this book. I actually read over 500 articles and book chapters. Did I mention that I'm a (cool) geek?

Are you ready? The next chapter is about motivation and why motivation is NOT a separate Psychological Key to Student Success. Let's go!

MOTIVATION – WHY IT IS NOT ONE OF THE PK2SS

When you finish this book, you will see that motivation has many sources and is different for everyone. Each Psychological Key to Student Success (PK2SS) is, in some way, related to motivation. Motivation is not one of the PK2SS but it is important enough to have its own brief chapter.

Perspectives and Theories

In psychology, motivation is viewed from many different perspectives. Some theories suggest that motivation comes from instincts. These are genetically-based, pre-programmed behavioral tendencies that help us survive. An example of an instinct is to run away from danger. Other theories describe motivation in terms of needs which are requirements a person must fulfill. Examples of needs are eating and sleeping. Obviously, there is a relationship between instincts and needs for behaviors related to survival. For example, we have a need to eat. If we do not meet this need, we will die. Our instinct, therefore, is to find and consume food. An animal's instinct might be to kill another animal for food whereas our instinct, as it has evolved over time, is to simply walk to the refrigerator and snarf down whatever we want. Instincts and needs motivate basic behaviors.

Abraham Maslow is a famous person in psychology who connected the ideas of motivation and needs. He suggested that our motivation is guided by a hierarchy of needs, where basic needs like hunger must be met before 'higher' needs such as achieving our personal potential. Feel free to Google "Maslow's Hierarchy of Needs" if you are curious.

Another significant point of view related to motivation comes from the behavioral perspective in psychology. Most famously, B. F. Skinner promoted the view that we learn to do (and not do) certain behaviors based on the rewards and punishments we receive. Building on the ideas of E. L. Thorndike, Skinner demonstrated that rewards increase the chance we will do a behavior again but punishment decreases the chance we will do a behavior again. You understand this already because your parents used rewards and punishments to teach you what to do and what not to do.

Most relevant to you here is motivation related to school achievement. In 1938, psychologist Henry Murray suggested that people have a "need to achieve." He said this is our desire "to overcome obstacles, to exercise power, [and] to strive to do something difficult as well as and as quickly as possible."[1] Research by David McClelland and John Atkinson expanded on this idea. McClelland explained that we "approach" what we want because of a strong need for achievement. Can you think of a personal example of a goal you set for yourself because you really wanted to achieve something? John Atkinson agreed but added we have an equally important and opposite need called the "need to avoid failure."[2,3] That need leads us to move away from, or "avoid," what we do not want. Can you think of a personal example of a time when you tried to make sure something *did not* happen (such as looking "stupid" or getting in trouble)?

Unfortunately, the motivation to avoid failure has some unfavorable outcomes.[4] For example, trying to avoid failure (you will read about this in PK2SS #3) can reduce the pursuit of your goals as well as decrease your self-esteem, personal control, and life satisfaction. The motivation to avoid failure also reduces self-regulation (you will read about this in PK2SS #6), college persistence, and grade point average.[5] Students who are most strongly motivated to protect themselves against failure are also most likely to abdicate (i.e., not take) responsibility for their failures and are more likely to blame others.[6,7] All that stuff should sound bad because it is!

Another interesting perspective in psychology is the "theory of planned behavior."[8] From this perspective, achievement is a combination of how hard you are willing to try (i.e., your intentions), your ability to actually do a behavior (called volitional control), and the situation. Situations and events come up in life that will change your intentions, your motivation, and your ability to do something. Anyone who decided to have children knows this! And last, the theory explains that social pressure impacts your intentions, and that also influences your motivation. Here is an example: I have worked with many students who intend to study when they get home from school or work. However, the situation at home is difficult because they have kids. Even though they really mean to study, they aren't always able to because caring for their children is the first priority.

Intrinsic and Extrinsic Motivation

Psychology often distinguishes between two types of motivation – intrinsic and extrinsic. I want to make sure the difference is clear and understandable.

> Intrinsic motivation is your desire to do something simply for its own sake. Intrinsic motivation comes from within you and is self-determined. An example from my life was learning to

fly. I got my private pilot's license simply because I wanted to. I love aviation.

Extrinsic motivation is your desire to gain a reward (or avoid a punishment) for doing something. Extrinsic motivation comes from outside you and is often described as "a means to an end." An example of this might be going to school in order to get a higher paying job.

Both types of motivation have a significant impact on your desire to approach good outcomes as suggested by David McClelland, and avoid bad outcomes as suggested by John Atkinson. As an example, if you simply love feeling knowledgeable about things, intrinsic motivation will lead you to study hard. At the same time, the extrinsic motivation to have a higher paying job (approach) and get out of poverty (avoid) will lead you to study hard. You will read, study, and complete assignments because you have an expectation about attaining a certain outcome and you then control your behavior as you pursue that outcome.[9]

Another interesting thing is that some aspects of the school environment can actually decrease your motivation![10] Consider these three examples:

a) Being rewarded for doing something you enjoy can reduce intrinsic motivation. For example, if drawing is very personal and fulfilling, being told over and over that your drawings are good sometimes takes away from the enjoyment of it.
b) Deadlines can reduce intrinsic motivation by increasing pressure and making what you like to do feel like something you have to do.

c) Being evaluated (tested) can reduce intrinsic motivation. For example, if you enjoy writing poetry, being critiqued can take away from your enjoyment of creative writing.

Before you run off and blame school for taking away your motivation, let me tell you that your perception is very important here. If you perceive rewards, deadlines, and evaluation as "controlling," you may feel less intrinsically motivated. "When controlled, whether by events or contexts outside themselves or by their own orientations to experience conditions as controlling, people tend to learn less well."[11] Basically that quotation means that if you are controlled by a person or circumstances, <u>or if you THINK you are being controlled</u>, you won't learn as well. Your intrinsic motivation largely depends "on how [a reward] affects perceived self-determination and perceived competence."[12]

You can't MAKE your classes or your teachers better in terms of the rewards, deadlines, or evaluations given. Some classes and teachers are not very engaging or interesting, I'm sorry to say. However, what others do or don't do is not our focus here. Our focus is on what YOU can do. You can control your perception of events and the environment. You may not get to choose your assignments but how and when you do them is up to you. You can't choose your exams but you can choose how to study for them. Even though you get to choose your courses, you can't choose how the courses are taught or the personality of the instructor. But, no matter what, you can choose what you focus on in terms of "This is ok," versus "This sucks." That simple change in thinking can increase the amount of control you have over your motivation!

This is one of the many ways this book will be useful to you. It will show you **HOW TO THINK** so that you don't suffer a loss of motivation due to circumstances, like boring teachers and bad evaluations that are beyond your control. This book will help you focus on what you can influence (your thinking) and how to influence it effectively.

There is a lot of good news about motivation and you're going to read all about it in the **Psychological Keys to Student Success (PK2SS)**! As I mentioned before, each PK2SS addresses your level of motivation in some way, shape, or form. Are you ready? Follow me as we explore the ways YOU are going to become a better student.

PK2SS #1 – BELIEFS & MINDSET

The beliefs you hold about learning are the first place you must look to understand your level of learning and achievement. "At its core, student success is determined by the attitudes and behaviors of individual students."[1] Did you catch that? Did ya? Developing a positive perception of yourself as a learner, and of the learning environment, is an important factor in deep learning.[2]

Imagine that a friend says to you, "It doesn't matter what I do. I can't learn this stuff. It's too hard. I'm just stupid." Prior to an exam, how will his belief about the material and his intelligence affect his approach to studying? Imagine that you run into another student who says, "I don't understand why people ask so many questions in class. The instructor gave us the information. That's it. It is what it is. I hate it when people try to complicate things with stupid 'what if' questions." If she believes that everything is black and white and that considering different viewpoints is useless, how will it affect how she studies?

It amazes me what many teachers and schools fail to teach. Many teachers don't come right out and tell you to consider your beliefs about education, knowledge, and learning. They frequently have you discuss your beliefs about "hot" topics such as discrimination, religion, culture, public policy, and sexual orientation. Very few teachers stress the importance of your personal beliefs about knowledge and learning. Really, how do people learn? How do YOU learn? What is knowledge and what do you believe it means to be knowledgeable? Let's delve into this and explore the importance of your beliefs!

Epistemological Beliefs

Epistemological beliefs are your beliefs about knowledge and learning. "Epistemological" can be a tricky word to pronounce (try this: Ah-pi-stem-ah-logical). These beliefs begin to develop when we are children. Young children have simple beliefs about knowledge and learning. They tend to believe that knowledge is absolute; it is about knowing "facts" and adults are experts who give them the facts. As we get older, many people begin to develop epistemological beliefs that reflect the fact that knowledge and learning are things that are complex and develop slowly over time. Sometimes not knowing is knowledge!

In my experience, when you try to learn something new and unfamiliar, especially if it is complex, it is common to try and just memorize the "facts." It is as if we are naturally trying to simplify complicated material. But, as you know, that doesn't always work because some things really are complicated!

Educational psychologist Marlene Schommer has researched epistemological beliefs and identified four aspects: innate ability, quick learning, simple knowledge, and certain knowledge.[3] Each aspect is like a dimension that ranges from naïve (simple) to sophisticated. The diagram you see on the next page is a summary from an article written in 2005.[4]

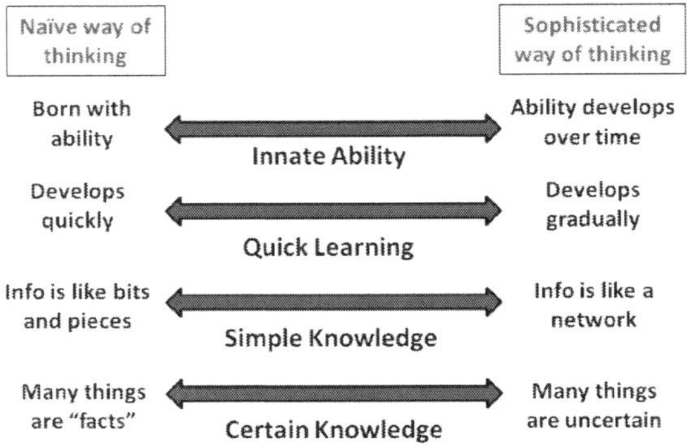

Here is an example from my teaching experience. In psychology, we study human thoughts and emotions which are affected by many different factors and situations. There are no equations for our thoughts and emotions. That kind of ambiguity (i.e., when something unclear or can be understood in many different ways) makes psychology difficult for students who believe that knowledge is simply about facts. If you believe that knowledge is like rules that do not change (i.e., knowledge is absolute), courses like psychology, philosophy, and ethics may frustrate you.

Epistemological beliefs affect your approach to every class you take, every book you read, every moment you study, and every exam you complete. Stop and consider the four aspects of epistemological beliefs for a class you are taking (or one you took in the past). Maybe you want to consider your beliefs about knowledge and learning for a math class. Perhaps you are taking a math class and a history class. Compare your epistemological beliefs for both. For example, maybe you think that math is an ability you are born with (or without) but you believe that learning about history is something that can improve over time. Maybe you think math is something you 'get' or you 'don't get' but that history is something you can catch onto. Is math about facts or is it ambiguous? How about history? Understanding these beliefs about knowledge and learning will help explain your approach to different classes, and it will also give you insight into your overall approach to school.

How Epistemological Beliefs Affect You – Some Research

Schommer's research demonstrated that students who believe that learning is quick and absolute in nature were more likely to draw overly simplistic conclusions when reading and do more poorly on tests.[5] Conversely, students who believed that learning is gradual had higher GPA's.[6] Schommer and one of her colleagues found that students who believe that ability can improve over time valued education and were more likely to persist when they encountered academic challenges.[7]

Recent research demonstrated that students who believe learning ability is something they are born with (or without) used fewer strategies "to connect their prior knowledge with new knowledge that is to be learned" and they did not "think critically about the information that they [were] processing."[8] Students who have more sophisticated epistemological beliefs (i.e., the right side of the chart) showed more effort and persistence.[9] Epistemological beliefs also influence achievement goal orientations, the third PK2SS you will learn about.

Beyond Schommer's Work

I am going to extend this discussion of epistemological beliefs beyond those mentioned thus far. Let's consider other common beliefs students have. For each, decide what you believe and then think about whether the belief helps you or hurts you.

Your Learning History

Everyone has positive and negative learning experiences in school. Those experiences, combined with your current educational goals, contribute to your beliefs and expectations about school and your academic abilities. How do beliefs about your abilities matter? Here is an example. A study of 253 university students in a macroeconomics course showed that those who had a lower GPA were more likely to overestimate their exam performance. However, having a higher GPA, higher ACT scores, and previous experience with the topic all reduced the tendency to overestimate ability.[10] This means that having accurate beliefs about your ability is very influential on your academic performance. Are your beliefs about your academic abilities accurate? We will consider this again in PK2SS #4.

"Easy" Classes

I'm sure you have taken a class and thought, "This will be easy." Many college students, when choosing elective classes, try to manage their schedules by selecting classes they hope will be less challenging to offset the workload of their required, harder classes. For example, some students who have never taken a psychology class before believe that psychology is "all common sense." After the first exam they realize this belief was very inaccurate. They spend the rest of the semester trying to recover from doing poorly on the first exam. Your beliefs about classes will influence how seriously you take them!

What Classes "Should" Be Like

What about your approach to learning in a class? If you believe that a class or instructor does not fit with your goals or your preferred learning style, you might experience negative emotions such as boredom or anxiety. These feelings can distract you and lead to lower performance.[11] A common example occurs when a student thinks that college classes should have a lot of discussions, group work, and projects. When that student enrolls in an introductory course that is lecture-based, he may start to think over and over about how the class is "pointless" and "stupid" and "boring" and how the teacher sucks. That kind of belief can be a big internal distraction, and it is entirely unnecessary.

What Teachers Should Be Like

What should and shouldn't teachers do? Your beliefs about this will affect your willingness to learn. Should teachers simply give out facts or should they challenge your beliefs too? What if teachers suggest things that are contrary to your religious or personal beliefs? Is that a sticking point you want to argue about or are you prepared to consider different perspectives as part of the educational process? Questions like these help you examine your epistemological beliefs. No matter how hard a teacher works to make a class interesting, how much a teacher knows about a topic, or how many different teaching strategies the teacher uses, it is your perception of the teacher, teaching strategies, and topics that matter most. The teacher could be awesome (like me) but if you don't like him/her or if you don't care about the class, it doesn't matter what the teacher is like. That's entirely on you (and how you think)!

How to Study

Another important belief relates to how to study for different types of exams. Many students adjust how they study based on the type of examination they expect to take and based on their belief about what the instructor expects of them on an exam.[12,13] Here is an example of this from my teaching experience: students treat multiple choice exams like they will be easy. They do not study as hard because they expect to recognize the correct answer from the answer choices. This is another very faulty expectation! Multiple choice questions can be very tricky because the choices may be similar. Relying on recognition alone often leads students to feel like the possibilities are all correct. Don't you just hate it when that happens? Well, guess what – you did it to yourself!

A 2009 research study asked 177 undergraduate students about their studying habits. Eighty-four percent reported simply rereading material as a studying strategy and 55% reported rereading was their preferred strategy. A much more effective strategy is to practice recalling the information (i.e., close your book and try to remember what you read). Only 11% used this method and only 1% said it was the preferred strategy. Another great studying strategy is to self-test but only 18% of the students reported this strategy as part of their studying.[14]

One studying tip I give students is to imagine that you arrive late for an exam. Everyone is gone and you catch me as I'm leaving the class. You apologize and ask if you can still take the exam. I tell you to meet me in my office in ten minutes. You arrive and thank me again. I say, "No problem." Then I say, "Are you ready? I am going to ask you questions. Just tell me the answers." Right then, you will likely have an 'OMG' moment. I'm not giving you the multiple choice exam. I'm giving you an oral exam!

In that scenario, if you would have known the exam was oral and not multiple choice, you probably would have prepared/studied differently. That simple realization reflects that you have different beliefs about different kinds of exams, and those beliefs guide how you study. I suggest that you study for all exams like you will have to explain everything to the professor. You will study much, much better!!

Time

Are you busy and, like so many others, believe there are simply not enough hours in the day? Do you believe that studying for easy classes should take only a little time but studying for harder classes will take longer? Do your expectations for how much time you have available to study match your professors' expectations about how much time is required to do well?

Please consider this statement about time: "According to both first-generation and traditional students, their time commitments inevitably reflected the amount of time that they had available, rather than the amount of time it would take to master the course material."[15] So, are you fitting college into your existing schedule or are you making college the main priority in your schedule? From the perspective of a college prof, I respect whatever students decide about their time and availability. However, your decisions about time do not change the expectations and requirements in college courses. The time you have and the effort you give are compared to the standards in the courses; profs don't lower the standards to accommodate your schedule.

Your Belief About the Value of Education

Your motivation to achieve is influenced by your perception of the value of education. This is important not just in your overall perception of education, but in each and every class you take. Researchers named Valentine, DuBois, and Cooper explained that your sense of the value of classes is made up of four parts: how important you think the class is, how interesting you find the material, how useful you think the material is, and any costs or problems associated with taking the class.[16] This means that HOW YOU THINK about the value of classes influences your motivation in those classes.

Wrapping Up Epistemological Beliefs

Whatever your beliefs are, the ones that stand out to you are most likely to influence how you approach school. In the words of Icek Ajzen, "these salient beliefs...are considered to be the prevailing determinants of a person's intentions and actions."[17] That is an eloquent way of saying that your beliefs are one of the main factors that influence what you do in school.

Mindset – A Type of Beliefs

Psychologist Carol Dweck researches and teaches about "implicit theories of intelligence." An implicit theory is your belief about how changeable intelligence is. Students who believe that intelligence can be developed and increased have an "incremental theory" of intelligence. This is more commonly called a "growth mindset." Alternatively, students who believe that intelligence is unchangeable have an "entity theory of intelligence." This is more commonly called a "fixed mindset."

There appears to be a pretty even split between people who hold growth mindsets and those who hold fixed mindsets (40% growth mindset; 40% fixed mindset; 20% undecided).[18] What do you believe? Is your intelligence is something you can improve (growth mindset) or do you believe your intelligence is something you're born with (fixed mindset)? Research has shown there are advantages associated with having a growth mindset. Students who have a growth mindset:

a) focus on the importance of learning for understanding, not just getting high grades;
b) see that making more effort is a sign of getting smarter, not a sign that something is too hard or that you're not smart enough;
c) feel that experiencing difficulty during a task is a sign of needing to work harder, not a lack of ability;
d) describe their performance (you will see this in PK2SS #2) in terms of their efforts and their use of strategies (both are changeable) rather than their intelligence;
e) hold a mastery achievement goal orientation (you will see this in PK2SS #3);
f) experience enjoyment in learning even when they are not naturally "good at" a topic;
g) are more likely to develop confidence (you will see this in PK2SS #4) as they learn, even if learning is a struggle;
h) feel less anxiety; and
i) retry things on which they didn't do well (students with a fixed mindset tend to avoid things they didn't do well on and, therefore, have trouble learning from mistakes).[19]

For our purposes here, you can think about the growth and fixed mindsets in terms of intelligence and you can also think of them in terms of other specific abilities. For example, are you good at math or do you suck at it? Right away you can see how your beliefs about your math abilities will influence your attitude toward math classes. What will happen if you think you suck at math and you are struggling with a math problem? Will things be different if you think you are good at math and you run into a tough math problem? There is a lot of research on the answer to these questions. One consistent finding is that a person's mindset varies from ability to ability. For example, you can have a growth mindset about your writing ability but a fixed mindset about your math ability: "If I practice writing, I know I'll get better at it. But, I don't think I'll ever be good at math."

Final Thoughts

Please understand that I "say" this with a smile: some students have odd beliefs about how learning occurs. I can assure you that learning does not magically come up through the classroom chair your butt is warming! Reading something only once rarely leads to significant, long-term learning. Joking with your friends while your books are open does not constitute a "study group." Studying while your kids terrorize the dog will likely provide little benefit. "Reading" while you text your BFF is pointless. Visiting your professor at the end of the semester and asking what you can do to pass, because you're failing, is totally useless (that one drives us nuts, by the way).

Becoming aware of your beliefs about knowledge, learning, intelligence, and specific school-related abilities can help you harness the power of helpful beliefs and work to change the unhelpful beliefs. Beliefs are like a filter through which all your experiences pass. If the beliefs are bad, your experience will be bad. If the beliefs are good . . . I'll let you finish that sentence. Keep reading and you will learn that epistemological beliefs and mindsets are connected to self-efficacy (PK2SS #4), metacognition (PK2SS #5), and self-regulated learning (PK2SS #6).

One last point: when teachers go on and on about "critical thinking," what they are doing, often without knowing it, is pressing you to examine your beliefs and understand the benefits of the right-hand column in the diagram shown earlier in this chapter. That column reflects some of the main ideas associated with critical thinking. Monique Boekaerts explained that "students should have the capacity and the inclination to question their intuitive beliefs, identify misconceptions, and replace them with a new explanatory framework."[20] That is what I'm trying to help you do here – question your beliefs about learning and develop beliefs that will serve you better in college.

Now that you are considering your beliefs and how they impact your performance in school, it is time to consider how you explain your performance. Why do you get good (or bad) grades on assignments, quizzes, and exams? It is time for PK2SS #2 – Attributions.

PK2SS #2 – ATTRIBUTIONS

Think of all the behaviors, our own and that of others, we try to explain. We try to answer "why" people do what they do and why they experience certain outcomes all the time. Why did you yell at your friend? Why do you eat too much? Why did you smile at that stranger? Why did that driver cut you off? Why did Mother Theresa help people? Why did your parents buy you birthday presents? WHY? WHY? WHY?

Related to school, think of reasons why you might get an A on an exam. Jot down as many possibilities as you can. You can do a similar exercise for why you might get a failing grade. There have to be reasons that explain why you get the results you do, right?

Every time you attempt to explain why a person (yourself or others) behaves a certain way, you are making an attribution. Every time you attempt to explain why a person (yourself or others) experiences some outcome, you are making an attribution. An attribution is your attempt to explain why a behavior or event happened. As we did with the first PK2SS (Beliefs & Mindset), we are focusing on **HOW YOU THINK**! How you make attributions reflects your beliefs, influences your motivation, and affects your emotions. It impacts everything about your school experience from your attendance to your studying habits to your grades.

According to Bernard Weiner, attributions are a "search for understanding" and a "spring for action."[1] In trying to explain achievement-related successes and failures, students evaluate their "level of ability, the amount of effort that was expended, the difficulty of the task, and the magnitude and direction of experienced luck."[2] In other words, when you get a grade on something in school, you consider your ability, effort, how hard the test or assignment was, and luck when trying to explain why you got that grade. Do those things sound familiar? Do you think about your ability and effort when you get a grade on something? Do you consider how hard an exam was when you try to explain the grade you received? Do you consider luck or other circumstances?

Weiner suggested and studied three aspects of attributions: locus, stability, and control.[3] Let's have a look at each.

The locus aspect of an attribution can be *internal or external*. When you make an attribution with an internal locus, you are saying that the cause of the behavior or event comes from within the person. For example, you got a D on the exam because of something you did (or didn't do), such as not studying enough, or because of your personal qualities, such as not being smart enough. When you make an attribution with an external locus, you are saying that the cause of the behavior or event comes from outside the person. For example, you got a D on the exam because the instructor didn't allow enough time or the exam was too hard.

The stability aspect of an attribution can be *stable or unstable*. When you make a stable attribution, you are saying that the cause of the behavior or event is unlikely to change across situations or over time. For example, you got a D on the exam because you are stupid ("stupid" doesn't change overnight). When you make an unstable attribution, you are saying that the cause of the behavior or event is likely to change depending on the situation or over time. For example, you got a D on the exam because you were tired.

The control aspect of an attribution can be *controllable or uncontrollable*. When you attribute a behavior or event to controllable factors, you are saying that the cause of the behavior or event is something the person can influence. For example, you got a D on the exam because you chose to not attend lectures and missed important information. When you attribute a behavior or event to uncontrollable factors, you are saying that the cause of the behavior or event is something the person cannot influence. For example, you got a D on the exam because it was scheduled on a day when you had two other exams.

Guess what. Our attributions can be a combination of all three aspects. In fact, each example above actually represents all three aspects of attributions. Consider the example of an exam that is scheduled on a day when you had two other exams. When you attribute your low grade to the exam schedule, you are right; you had no control over it. That attribution is also external (i.e., the schedule is outside of you) and unstable (i.e., it is unlikely that having three exams back-to-back-to-back on one day will happen again in the future).

At the beginning of this chapter I asked you to generate reasons why you might get a good grade on an exam. I also asked you to explain why you might get a bad grade. What explanations did you come up with? Let's say you attribute poor performance to "being stupid." In terms of the three aspects of attributions outlined by Weiner, "being stupid" is internal, stable, and uncontrollable. "Stupidity" is a personal quality (internal), it is unlikely to change quickly (stable), and a lot of people believe it isn't something you can do a lot about (it is uncontrollable IF you believe that intelligence is primarily influenced by genetics).

This shows one way that the first two PK2SS are connected. If you hold a fixed mindset about intelligence (i.e., you believe intelligence is unchangeable), you are more likely to attribute success to being smart and failure to being stupid. Either way, the attribution is internal, stable, and uncontrollable. If you are on the smart end of this judgment, you will feel successful and be motivated to do well again in the future. However, in our example of doing poorly and attributing it to "stupidity," your feelings will be unpleasant and your subsequent motivation will be reduced.

Now assume that you hold a growth mindset (i.e., you believe intelligence can change) and you do poorly on an exam. Here, your belief is that intelligence is unstable (that it can change). In this case, you may still attribute your grade to "stupidity" but you will be motivated to work harder because you believe you can be smarter. The attribution is still internal but now it is changeable and controllable based on your belief that you can get smarter.

The third aspect of attributions, control, highlights the connection between behavior and outcomes as well as how much you believe you are capable of doing the necessary behavior.[4] A study of 524 college students found that students higher in perceived academic control tried harder, reported higher motivation, used more self-monitoring strategies, experienced less boredom and anxiety, and got higher grades.[5] In other words, if you think grades are something you can control, you do better. Research has also shown that students who are low in perceived academic control are less likely to benefit from quality teaching.[6] That means if you tend to blame academic problems on everything and everyone else, it won't matter how good the teacher is. You won't benefit from good teaching unless you take responsibility for your learning and the results you get.

I hope you see how beliefs and attributions are closely linked. I also hope you see that some attributions can be inspiring while others can be very unmotivating. Generally speaking, it is better to make internal attributions for success and failure. Yes, BOTH! Why? Internal attributions put you "in the driver's seat." This is what is meant by the term 'personal responsibility.' If you do well, take credit for it! If you do poorly, own it! This is what Julian Rotter (1966) called "locus of control," and it is the first aspect of attributions.[7] The key question: is what happens to you in school up to you, or is up to things outside you?

Accepting responsibility for poor performance can be a little tricky in terms of attributions. As you already saw, saying you are stupid is a form of "owning" poor performance but that can be unmotivating if you have a fixed mindset. However, saying that you didn't try hard enough or that you didn't practice enough is something you can control. Lack of effort or practice is clearly changeable. That can motivate you. The key to this distinction is to make internal attributions that are controllable. When you do poorly on something, it is much better to attribute that result to unstable and controllable factors such as effort, because it "allows the student to protect his self-worth [and] it also helps the student to see a way to avoid failure in the future."[8] That is, attributing poor performance to something you can control, such as making more effort or paying closer attention, means that you can reduce the chance of poor performance in the future; you can improve!

Taking credit for your success is internal and motivating. However, some students actually make external attributions for their successes. That's right. They don't take credit for their success. This can be helpful or unhelpful. If you get a lot of help and attribute your success to that help, it may just be a sign of gratitude and a recognition that you did well, in part, because of the help you got. Alternatively, some students who do well say, "The instructor just made an easy exam" or "I got lucky." The effect of these external attributions for success might reduce motivation by making you feel like you had nothing to do with your own success. This can also depend a lot on your cultural background. We will consider that in PK2SS #8.

When Are You Most Motivated to Understand "WHY?"

There are times and situations when you are more likely to actively think about why a behavior or event occurred. Students are more likely to be concerned with explaining why they get bad results. Doing poorly does not have to mean that you get an F; it can be that you achieve at a level that is lower than what you expected or hoped for.[9]

In addition to doing poorly, another time you are motivated to explain your results is when events are unexpected (good or bad), especially if the outcome or event is personally relevant. For example, when you get a grade that is lower than expected that outcome is experienced as poor, unexpected, and very personally relevant to your course grade. In that case, you will be motivated to explain WHY! With your understanding of attributions, what will happen if you attribute the lower-than-expected grade to stupidity? How about lack of effort? How would these attributions affect your feelings and subsequent motivation and behavior? Remember, saying you are stupid is unmotivating. Also remember that attributing a poor grade to lack of effort may upset you but is something you can readily change!

I just got through telling you that people are more likely to try and explain poor results. I'd like to suggest that you should also actively think about why you have success and that you should do it very intentionally. How can you repeat success if you don't examine and understand what you did (internal, controllable attribution) to achieve it? Always think about your successes and what you did to achieve them so that you can repeat them. At the same time you should consider situational factors so you can understand that what you did in one situation/class might not always work in a different situation/class. Pay attention to both the personal and situational factors.

Expectations and Your Attributions

There is another connection between your beliefs (PK2SS #1) and attributions. In a general sense, students who did well in high school enter college with an expectation that they will continue getting good grades. We considered this in PK2SS #1. That expectation (belief) has with it the attributional characteristic of stability: "I do well in school." If this describes how you think, how will you respond in college to getting a lower grade than what you wanted? If you say, "College is hard and I can't do it because all classes will be like this," that attribution will reduce your motivation. If you say, "I am smart because I did well in high school but I obviously need to do more in college," that internal attribution suggests you can do something about the situation (it is changeable and controllable). That is much better for your motivation.

Clearly, your expectations (beliefs) influence how you explain your academic results. Research suggests that your expectations come from your ideas about your own ability and how much effort you plan to make,[10] how much your achievement efforts have been reinforced,[11] and social aspects of the school environment such as competition (how you stack up compared to others) and performance feedback.[12]

Emotions and Your Attributions

When we talk about our emotions as they relate to the outcomes we experience, there are basic reactions that are "outcome-dependent" and there are emotions that are "attribution-dependent."[13, 14] Outcome-dependent emotions are the feelings you get right when something happens. Attribution-dependent emotions are the feelings you get after you try to explain why something happened.

Here is an example. When you get a paper back with a big A+ at the top, you will feel happy. That is the simple, outcome-dependent emotion. When you then think about how hard you worked on the paper, you may experience attribution-dependent emotions such as pride, satisfaction, and confidence. However, if you attribute your good grade to luck, perhaps the attribution-dependent emotion will be relief instead of pride. These emotions will influence your subsequent motivation and behavior differently.

Now imagine that you get your paper back and it has a big, red D at the top. Your outcome-dependent emotion may be anger or anxiety. Then you have to make an attribution. If you attribute getting a D to stupidity, you may feel hopeless and sad. In that case, you may be motivated to avoid academic tasks (this can contribute a lot to procrastination, especially for those who fear failure). If, however, you attribute the D to an internal, unstable, and controllable factor like a lack of effort, you may feel disappointed in yourself and, therefore, be motivated to do better next time. THIS ALL HINGES ON HOW YOU THINK!

Attribution Errors

The confidence you have in your academic skills is important, but it must also be accurate! Thinking you are a better student than you actually are can create significant attributional errors (like blaming low grades on a teacher). Similarly, thinking you are a weak student when you are actually capable can lead to errors too, such as thinking you are stupid when you are not.

When it comes to your beliefs and attributions, I want you to develop greater self-awareness and the ability to assess yourself accurately. Attributions are only helpful and great sources of learning and motivation to the extent they are realistic and accurate. For example, attributions of success will not be believable if you keep failing, and attributions of low effort for failure will be meaningless if you try really hard but still fail.[15]

In order to make accurate attributions about a behavior or event, you need to consider both personal characteristics and aspects of the situation. Consider the following two scenarios:

a) You consistently arrive late to class and the teacher finally tells you that your behavior is disruptive and unacceptable.
b) A classmate you don't know consistently arrives late to class and the teacher finally tells the student that his behavior is disruptive and unacceptable.

Here is the key question: to what do you attribute your own consistent tardiness (i.e., being late) and to what do you attribute your classmate being consistently tardy?

In the above example, you are more likely to attribute your own tardiness to situational factors such as bad traffic or having back-to-back classes. You are more likely to attribute the same behavior of your classmate to his/her personal characteristics such as being disrespectful or inconsiderate.

There are three attributional biases that are common in Western psychology. The first attributional bias is called the self-serving bias. It says we are more likely to attribute our success to personal qualities but attribute our bad behavior to situational factors. For example, when you get an A you are more likely to say you are a great student, but when you get a D you are more likely to say that the test was too hard.

The second bias, called the fundamental attribution error, occurs when we judge the behavior of others. We are more likely to attribute other people's bad behavior or results to their personal qualities and are less likely to consider the situation. For example, when a classmate fails an exam, you are more likely to say that the she is "dumb" instead of considering that she has two jobs and doesn't have time to study as much as she wants.

The third bias is called the actor-observer bias. When you are actively part of a situation, you will make different attributions about behavior than if you are an observer of the situation. For example, when you give a presentation (i.e., you are the "actor") and you feel nervous, you might attribute your nervousness to the instructor looking at you and writing stuff down or your classmates whispering and giggling. That is, you make an external attribution for your nervousness. You explain your nervousness to be the result of what is happening outside of you. However, when someone else is doing a presentation (i.e., you are an "observer" now) and looks nervous, you are more likely to attribute her nervousness to her lack of preparation or her shyness. You make an internal attribution for her nervousness. You say she is nervous because of something about her. It is exactly the same situation but our attributions change depending on whether we are in the situation or if we are watching the situation.

Final Thoughts

As you can see, making attributions can be complex and prone to errors. However, I hope this PK2SS has you considering how you explain your behavior and the results you get. It will really influence your motivation and feelings. When you think about your personal beliefs (PK2SS #1) and your style of making attributions (PK2SS #2), you can see the importance of HOW YOU THINK. We are building up your psychological knowledge and skills to make you a more successful student. Next we are going to consider your goals!

PK2SS #3 – ACHIEVEMENT GOALS & INTEREST

If I asked you what an achievement goal is, you might say, "It is what a person wants to accomplish in school." Does that sound about right? Well, believe it or not, an achievement goal has become a tricky thing for psychologists to define. Leave it to psychology to take two terms that are easy to understand (achievement and goals), mash them together, and make a complicated term. Because this concept is one of the Psychological Keys to Student Success, I'll help you navigate through the mess psychology has made. Yes, I'm making fun of my own discipline! Please bear with me as I tell you what psychology says about this concept. You are about to read some complicated definitions. However, as is my goal in this book, I will try to help you break the information down into something useful.

Goals

Here are some general definitions of goals. Goals "represent students' perceptions and beliefs about the purposes of academic achievement."[1] They move you toward a specific, desired outcome, establish definitions of generally acceptable performance, and help you regulate your efforts (such as increasing motivation and focus while avoiding distractions).[2] Goals also help you know the criteria for self-evaluation.[3]

I hope that didn't sound too bad and that you noticed words from the first two PK2SS and the chapter on motivation. Did you notice the word "beliefs?" Did you notice the word "outcome?" Did you notice the word "motivation?" Goals allow you to define what you want and how to get it. Goals also suggest what you need to think about in terms of how well you do in pursuit of the goal.

Achievement Goals

Achievement goals are not simply about getting a good outcome; they are about how you define competence.[4] They are about your motivation to become skilled at something. Psychologist Carol Ames defined an achievement goal as "an integrated pattern of beliefs, attributions, and affect that produces the intentions of behavior and that is represented by different ways of approaching, engaging in, and responding to achievement type activities."[5]

I don't blame you if you're thinking, "OMG! What does that mean?" Well, hang on. Let's pick that definition apart and you'll see why it is useful. Notice right away that the first two things she mentioned are the first two Psychological Keys to Student Success – beliefs and attributions! Basically the quotation says your beliefs and attributions lead you to do achievement-related behaviors such as enrolling in school, going to classes, studying for exams, and learning from feedback. See, that wasn't so bad.

Are you ready to really shake your head? Here's another definition: an achievement goal is a "future-focused cognitive representation that guides behavior to a competence-related end state that the individual is committed to either approach or avoid."[6] WHAT? LOL! Psychologists are funny. They don't always put things in terms that people can actually understand (and I think they need to go outside and play more often). Well, let's pick that definition apart too and find something useful. In that quotation, achievement goals are given a number of qualities.

a) They help you focus on what you want to accomplish in the future. They give you a purpose. That sounds like a goal, right? Ok, so far, so good!
b) They are something you think about and can "see" in your mind (that is the "cognitive representation" part). They give you a vision in your mind about your future.
c) They lead you to try and develop skills. You gotta know how to do stuff, right?
d) They might lead you to avoid some things too. Don't get hung up on the "avoid" part. I promise to explain that later. Keep reading!

Here is one last definition. Paul Pintrich suggested that our achievement goal orientations represent our "beliefs about purposes, competence, success, ability, effort, errors, and standards."[7] He was basically saying that our achievement goal orientations are a set of beliefs. So, is it possible to consider this third PK2SS as part of the first PK2SS? Well, maybe. Hold that thought for the moment; let's look at different types of achievement goals and see how they affect your approach to classes, and school in general.

Types of Achievement Goal Orientations

There are two general types of achievement goals students can adopt when they take a class. They are called mastery goals and performance goals. You have a mastery goal orientation when you want to become competent by learning new knowledge and skills. You have a performance goal orientation when you want to demonstrate competence compared to others. The key distinction is that in a mastery orientation you want to BE competent, but in a performance orientation you want to APPEAR competent.

Another way of describing the difference between mastery

and performance goal orientations comes from the seminal work of Carol Dweck and Ellen Leggett.[8] They suggested that mastery-focused students want to **improve** ability whereas performance-focused students want to **prove** their ability. Mastery oriented students want to increase their ability; performance oriented students are concerned with whether or not their existing ability is adequate. In a mastery orientation, students are developing knowledge and skills and comparing progress to their existing knowledge and skill. In a performance orientation, students are comparing their knowledge and skill to the knowledge and skill of others.

Here is an example of how these goal orientations can help you or hurt you. First, consider the mastery goal orientation. Let's pretend your present knowledge in psychology is pretty low. You are totally new to the subject. You focus and work hard because you want to improve your knowledge. You study hard and, after a few weeks, you notice that your understanding has increased a lot. Even though you haven't achieved the ultimate level of knowledge and skill you are striving for, you are improving. That is motivating so you keep pursuing more knowledge. Your point of reference is your own knowledge and skill and that it is improving.

Now let's pretend you have a performance goal orientation. Your focus is on grades and how your grades compare to the grades others are getting. Right now, let's say your general knowledge in psychology is a 3/10. You notice that others are 7/10. You will feel motivated to beat their scores. To be completely honest, that can be very motivating. In that example, the performance goal can serve you well.

Let me show you when a performance goal is a problem. Consider again that your knowledge level in psychology is a 3/10 but the people you are comparing yourself to are only a 4/10. You don't have to work very hard or know very much to beat them. So, when you get yourself up to a 5/10, you are the BEST! You don't know much but you are better than everyone else! Once you are the "best" you won't be as motivated to continue learning and developing. That is one down side to a performance goal orientation.

Another potential problem with a performance goal orientation is that comparing yourself to others might make you worry about appearing unskilled or incompetent. That can make you avoid challenging tasks and evaluation (remember I said goals can actually lead you to avoid things too).

Benefits of the Mastery Goal Orientation

Students with a mastery goal orientation have some desirable characteristics. They want to learn for the sake of learning (intrinsic motivation). This often relates to having more interest in an area (or for learning in general). They seek out and enjoy a challenge and will keep trying when things are difficult. They believe that effort leads to ability. They are also likely to learn from the feedback they receive, even when the feedback is "negative."

Related to PK2SS #1, beliefs, students with a mastery goal orientation are more likely to have a growth mindset. Students with a mastery goal orientation are likely to experience more positive emotions associated with learning, be more open to working collaboratively with other students, and be more open to sharing and understanding opinions.[9] They tend to make better attributions about successes and failures. That is, they see effort as the path to learning and see any failures as a sign they used the wrong learning strategy, not as an indication of incompetence.[10]

Related to PK2SS #4 which you will read about next, students with a mastery goal orientation are more likely to "interpret feedback in terms of their progress, thereby supporting their self-efficacy."[11] That means feedback, good and bad, helps them feel more confident.

Researchers named Heidi Grant and Carol Dweck conducted a series of studies and found a number of benefits associated with a mastery goal orientation. Mastery oriented students:

a) viewed "negative" feedback about their work as an opportunity to learn and improve. As you already learned, attributions (PK2SS #2) are important. Thinking that you can improve is more motivating than thinking your difficulties are because of low intelligence.
b) appeared to benefit from having more interest and intrinsic motivation for learning.
c) demonstrated better planning and more persistence toward their desired academic outcomes.[12]

Students with a mastery goal orientation have, overall, a more positive attitude toward learning. They believe that effort will lead to success.[13,14] Positive correlations have been found between mastery goals and interest, effort, cooperation, help-seeking, self-regulated learning, and the use of better learning strategies.[15,16] Research has demonstrated a relationship between mastery goals and the experience of positive emotions including pride and hope; mastery goals can also buffer students against negative emotions like boredom, anger, hopelessness, and shame.[17]

Performance Orientation – Some Ups and Downs

This orientation has a number of interesting facets; it is not just one, straight-forward thing. Students with a performance goal orientation may experience different kinds of motivation. One type of motivation is to appear competent and intelligent. With an appearance motivation you may not care about how others have done on an assignment or exam as long as you have impressed an audience (such as the instructor). The other type of motivation is what we call "normative." This means that a student is concerned with comparing his/her abilities to that of others. With normative motivation, you would actively compare your grade with how other students did. But, no matter how you explain it, both motivations express concern about being evaluated.[18]

Over many years of research, performance goals have been differentiated into performance-approach and performance-avoidance goals. If you have a performance-approach goal, you will be concerned with looking competent but you will tackle challenges like they are opportunities. This increases motivation, concentration, and intrinsic motivation. You will invest yourself in the activity. Alternatively, a performance-avoidance goal will leave you trying to not look incompetent or stupid. Challenges are seen as a threat. If something is difficult, you will try to protect yourself against failure and you are more likely to make up phony excuses when you do badly. You are more likely to be distracted, procrastinate, and/or give up. Sadly, the desire to avoid failure can be a very powerful motivator, one with many negative consequences.[19]

Andrew Elliot and Judith Harackiewicz did some interesting research on this approach and avoidance distinction. First, they found that students with mastery, performance-approach, and performance-avoidance goals all showed effort and ability on a task. That's right. All the students tried hard and were able to do the task given by the researchers. However, the researchers found that students with the performance avoidance orientation suffered significant costs. The fact that their motivation was to avoid failure seemed to take away their intrinsic motivation. They were less persistent when having trouble with a task and showed a tendency to focus more on themselves instead of the task. That was like a big internal distraction and it left them unable to enjoy the task in the same way as those with a mastery or performance-approach orientation.[20]

Here are some other interesting research findings. Fears and anxiety experienced by students with an avoidance orientation "cascade forward through time" and disrupt studying for exams, which negatively affects exam performance.[21] Students who begin a semester with the performance-approach goal orientation may actually shift to the performance-avoidance goal orientation if they do poorly on the first exam.[22] As well, students with the performance-avoidance orientation may have greater fear of failure and lower expectations about their own competence.[23] Students who fear failure actually end up focusing more on protecting their self-worth than striving to achieve.[24]

There is also research that shows students with the avoidance orientation actually select less challenging tasks in the first place. Students with a performance-avoidance goal orientation may experience more boredom, anger, anxiety, hopelessness, and shame and those negative emotions can lead to poorer academic achievement.[25,26]

One thing I notice in my classes when I explain goal

orientations is the look on some students' faces. I can see that they start to worry because they recognize a performance-avoidance orientation in themselves. If you are one of those students reading this right now, please DO NOT give up. Keep reading. There is good news coming.

Achievement Orientations – General or Specific?

You can have different achievement goals in different settings. For example, you might have a mastery orientation in chemistry simply because you have great interest in it. However, you might have a performance-avoidance orientation in your philosophy class because you consistently feel incompetent. As a result, you might participate fully in chemistry but skip philosophy class. You might study for many hours for a small chemistry quiz but procrastinate terribly for a big midterm exam in philosophy.

Now that you understand these achievement goal orientations better, which sounds most like your overall approach to school? Do you fall more toward the mastery or performance orientation? If you think you fall more toward the performance-avoidance orientation, keep reading. Simply reading this book is helping you develop thinking skills that match the mastery and performance-approach orientations! I'm pretty sneaky, huh? ☺

Can I Be a Combination of Orientations?

Absolutely! You can have aspects of a mastery goal orientation and a performance goal orientation at the same time, and even in the same class! Let me share a personal example from when I was getting my Bachelor's degree. I was really interested in my psychology classes and had a ton of intrinsic motivation to understand all the material. That is the mastery goal orientation. I was also competitive and wanted to "beat" everyone on assignments and exams. That is the performance-approach orientation. Together, those two goal orientations served me well. I received the Dean of Arts medal when I graduated with my Bachelor's degree. That means the school thought I was the coolest geek there (well, not quite but...lol).

Goal Orientations – Summary

I have read a ton of articles (geek) about achievement goal orientations. Some of the information is straight-forward. Most of it is complex. There is one take-home message I have for you: both mastery and performance-approach goals can be beneficial. The mastery orientation benefits are many and they are clear. However, we live in a competitive world. In cases of competition, a performance-approach orientation can help too. The key is that you develop both along with the judgment and flexibility to know when and how to use both to your advantage. It is also important to be aware of the fear of failure and likelihood of procrastination associated with the performance-avoidance orientation. It can be crippling but it is something you can change (remember the growth mindset)!

Interest

I'm sure you can think of topics you find interesting where the interest seems to come from inside you somewhere. I'm also sure you can think of topics that you find interesting in the moment but that you wouldn't pursue over the long term. Interest is part of both mastery and performance goals. Interest is also a great source of motivation to learn, and research has shown that interest is associated with being more engaged in learning, increased attention, positive emotions, and getting higher grades.[27,28]

Interest can be situational but it also seems to be a bit like an individual personality characteristic. When it is situational, your motivation comes from qualities of the topic/situation. When it is like a personality characteristic, motivation comes from inside you. A quick example from my own experience might help. I was drawn to psychology because of my general interest in understanding and helping people. That interest is just part of who I am (individual, intrinsically motivated interest). In any given psychology class, however, my situational interests varied. For example, I found information about schizophrenia fascinating in the moment but I was never interested beyond that.

Another example from my personal life relates to aviation. Ever since I was a kid, I have been interested in flight. I can't explain why. I just think that it is really cool! Back in 2000, I earned a private pilot's license. To get that license, I had to learn about many topics including engines and physics. I had zero interest in engines and physics. However, because they were part of aviation, I learned what I needed to in order to achieve the higher goal of being a licensed pilot. Learning about engines and physics actually became interesting simply because they were related to flying.

There is a lot of research about how teachers can trigger a student's interest.[29,30] The research shows that it is important for teachers to stimulate interest in students and to understand students' different learning styles. <u>But I did not write a book about what teachers and parents should do for you to be successful. I wrote a book for YOU about what YOU can do to be successful</u>. Our consideration of interest, therefore, must focus on YOUR role in your own level of interest in school. It is equally important for you to understand that "teachers have no influence over students' incoming personal interests."[31]

As I already explained, interest is one source of motivation that influences the goals you pursue and how and when you pursue them. Interest affects your feelings about a topic, how attentive you are during that topic, and how open you are to receiving feedback about your performance.

Suggestions

Here are some ideas about how you can create, maintain, and pursue your interests. I hate the idea of you sitting back waiting for someone or something else to "make" you interested in a topic, assignment, or class. That doesn't fit in either the mastery or the performance goal orientations. It also doesn't fit with personal responsibility.

Suggestion #1: Interest is a function of how much you "like" something, but it also relates to how useful and personally relevant you think it is. Teachers can try to point out the utility (i.e., the usefulness) and the meaningfulness about a topic but they don't know everything about you. They can't tell you exactly how to apply the topic to YOUR experience. They give examples but you must participate in connecting what you're learning in school to your own life and future. This requires thought and effort (important parts of a mastery orientation). Research shows that utility and interest are connected.[32] Therefore, always try to relate new information to your personal experience.

Sometimes the connections won't be obvious. Don't quit on an idea or dismiss it as irrelevant or boring or stupid just because you can't see its use or relevance in the moment. For example, I didn't fully realize the power of metaphors in high school English class. But, ten years later when I was counseling people, metaphors became very useful. I am glad I didn't dismiss them as useless!

Suggestion #2: I try very hard when I'm teaching to capture my students' interest. Once I have their interest, I try to help them maintain it. However, I cannot "make" interest happen (as explained a few paragraphs back) nor can I "make" you stay interested. My second suggestion relates to the first: you must participate. The best way to do this is to answer questions asked by the instructor and ask your own questions in class. Participation is a great way to develop and maintain interest.[33] You must be engaged! This is another quality of mastery oriented students because they want "meaning," not just the "answers" for the test.

Suggestion #3: This is based on the work of Roger Azevedo and is short, sweet, and to the point. You will be better able to generate interest if you have two things. First, you need time. Second, you need feelings of competence (i.e., efficacy).[34] So, try hard to not stretch yourself too thin by having a million things to do. It is hard to be interested in things when you are overwhelmed by all the stuff you "have to" do. Also make sure you carefully consider PK2SS #4,self-efficacy, which is coming up next!

Suggestion #4: Another important reason to try and develop some level of interest in all your classes is that it affects how much time you spend studying. In a series of three studies, Son and Metcalfe found that students allocate more study time to things they find interesting.[35] Let this tip also serve as a caution: just because you find it interesting and, therefore, study it more, doesn't necessarily mean it is important material. Study everything! Study everything well!

Final Thoughts

Did you benefit from thinking about these goal orientations and the ideas about interest? I certainly hope my explanations and examples helped you understand the academic quotations and definitions. Pause for a moment and think about what you are learning and how it relates to you (apply suggestion #1).

Now you are ready to learn about the importance of your confidence. In psychology, we refer to that as "self-efficacy" and it is PK2SS #4.

PK2SS #4 – SELF-EFFICACY

What are you good at? What activity or sport or hobby or job or class or...well, what are you good at?!?! Asked a slightly different way, in what things do you have confidence in your abilities? Are you pretty confident in your cooking ability? How about playing baseball? Maybe you are confident in your ability to make new friends or give a speech. What things related to school do you believe you do well? “Self-efficacy” is psychology’s term for the confidence you have in your ability to accomplish something. It is a sense of your own competence.

Let’s focus specifically on college success. In what school-related abilities do you have confidence? Math? Science? Art? History? Anatomy? Psychology? Computer programming? Drama? Languages? Do you have confidence in specific skills like taking notes, doing a research paper, organization, time management, and reading comprehension? Do you have a good vocabulary? How is your grammar? Teachers, tutors, and other books have a lot to say about studying skills and academic abilities like those. The question is, how effective will those skills be if you lack confidence?

Why is Self-efficacy Important?

How well you do, how hard you try, your choice of tasks, and your expectations and values are all influenced by your confidence.[1] If you hold stronger beliefs about your ability, you are more likely to set higher goals for achievement which can, in turn, increase your effort and persistence.[2,3] Confidence in your ability is a great source of motivation.[4] Students with greater academic self-efficacy are more likely to be engaged in an activity, persist, recover when things go poorly, achieve their goals, and achieve their goals at a higher level than students with lower levels of self-efficacy. [5,6,7] Albert Bandura (1994) stated "beliefs of personal efficacy can shape the course [of a person's life] by influencing the types of activities and environments" he/she chooses.[8]

In terms of what you are learning in this book, believing that "academic success is under [your] control" is a significant step toward becoming a self-regulated learner (you will read about that in PK2SS #6).[9]

Self-efficacy: It Depends

As you might have guessed, you can have a different level of confidence in everything from grammar to graduation! Self-efficacy depends on the situation, topic or skill you consider. As a personal example, I lack confidence in my ability to do complicated math, but if you give me a presentation to do, I have a lot of confidence in my ability. The funny thing is that confidence in your ability and your actual ability can be very different. Truthfully, although I don't have a lot of math efficacy, I got As in math throughout high school and college. And, just because I have confidence in my ability to do a presentation doesn't mean I'm the best at it.

In a 2004 review, out of 9 possible factors, academic self-efficacy was the best predictor of GPA.[10] Clearly, academic self-efficacy is extremely important. This is another example of the importance of HOW YOU THINK!

Self-efficacy: The Work of Albert Bandura

In 1977, Albert Bandura wrote a paper called "Self-efficacy: Toward a unifying theory of behavioral change." Within that paper were a number of significant ideas that became a springboard for decades of research about self-efficacy and motivation. Bandura described an efficacy expectation as "the conviction that [a person] can successfully execute the behavior required to produce the [desired] outcomes."[11] With efficacy we are talking about your belief that you can do the behavior (whether it gets you the result you want or not). Many students are confident that they can get a high GPA (i.e., desired outcome) but fail to do so. Others lack confidence in their academic ability (i.e., low efficacy) when they may, in fact, have the ability to do very well in school.

Albert Bandura explained that our sense of self-efficacy comes from four sources of information. I have added school-related examples to help you apply the ideas to your own experience.

Source 1: Experience

The first source of efficacy comes from your actual experiences. Let's say you write, for the very first time, a poem in a creative writing class. You receive a good grade and the teacher tells the class how good your poem is. As you write more poems, you continue to get positive feedback and good grades. You are having success. That success will likely increase the confidence you have in your creative writing ability. Now assume the opposite is happening in your architectural drafting class. You are getting low grades and negative feedback on your designs and drawings. Over time these "failures" will contribute to lower feelings of efficacy. Because writing poems and drawing schematics are different skills, you will probably develop high self-efficacy for creative writing and simultaneously hold low efficacy beliefs for architectural drafting. As explained by Bandura, "successes raise mastery expectations; repeated failures lower them," and repeated successes reduce the "negative impact of occasional failures."[12] Other researchers wrote, "before...students can begin to think about school learning playing a realistic role in their futures, they must begin experiencing consistent and meaningful success in school."[13]

Sometimes feelings of efficacy can spill over (generalize) to other settings and activities. High self-efficacy for creative writing might spill over to all written assignments (e.g., research papers, short stories, personal reflections), but it might not. There are many factors that contribute to how specific or general self-efficacy becomes based on learning experiences (too many to consider in this book). Simply remember that you can have different levels of efficacy for different school subjects, assignments, and activities.

There is an important link between your previous experiences, your self-efficacy, and your goals. That link is PK2SS #2, attributions. Bernard Weiner wrote that our "causal ascriptions for past performance are an important determinant of goal expectancies."[14] That means your efficacy and future goals are based much more on how you perceive your past experiences than the actual experiences themselves! For example, if you did well in high school but attribute your success to luck, you may still lack confidence in your ability. As such, you might set lower academic goals in college or worry a lot about doing poorly.

Source 2: Vicarious Experience

The second source of efficacy information comes from "vicarious experiences." Sometimes confidence in your ability increases or decreases based solely on seeing someone else do a behavior. For example, if you observe a classmate build a model of a house using popsicle sticks (something you've never done before), you might suddenly feel confident (i.e., develop efficacy) that you can do it too. Your feeling of confidence is not based on your own experience; it is based on what someone else did and experienced. Here's another example. Have you ever watched someone do a presentation and screw it up? Have you ever felt nervous or embarrassed "for" the person? You weren't doing the presentation so why did you feel nervous or embarrassed? Both are examples of vicarious experiences.

Just for a moment, let's consider the example of doing a presentation. Feeling nervous (or being downright afraid) to give a presentation is common for many students, but you can develop confidence in your ability to do a presentation by watching other students successfully complete a presentation. This is not as powerful as successfully doing a presentation yourself but it can help. This is part of how modeling and tutoring can be helpful; watching someone else succeed can help us build feelings of confidence. If you see someone else perform a behavior and estimate, "I can do that too," your efficacy can increase even though you haven't tried the behavior yourself. Bandura suggested that seeing many different people with many different skill levels try something and succeed is more beneficial than simply watching the teacher do it.[15,16]

Source 3: Persuasion

The third source of efficacy comes from verbal persuasion. Sometimes a bit of encouragement from someone you trust, love, or respect is enough to give you a little more confidence. Think of a person in your life who you might believe if he/she said to you, "I know you can do it. I think you're really good at it." Maybe that person is a parent or a teacher. Do you remember a time when you doubted your ability and a coach or a friend or a teacher gently encouraged you and you felt a little more confident? Have you ever done that for one of your friends or a family member? As it is with vicarious experiences, this is also not as powerful an influence on efficacy as succeeding at something. However, it can work wonders at times. For me, my mother has been a never-ending source of encouragement in everything I have done. Her support has helped me overcome fears and helped me achieve a lot of personal goals. I love you, Mom!! ☺

Source 4: Emotion

The fourth source of efficacy is your level of emotional arousal. In the face of a challenging task, such as a tough assignment, a presentation, or an important exam, you interpret your level of internal arousal as a cue about your confidence and skill. For example, if you feel really nervous, you might think you lack skill or knowledge. That interpretation lowers your sense of efficacy. Alternatively, if you feel pretty calm (i.e., low arousal), you are more likely to interpret that as a sign of confidence. Think of how this relates to PK2SS #2, attributions. If you attribute your "nerves" to a normal part of taking an exam, you probably won't worry as much. If, however, you attribute your "nerves" to a lack of academic skills, you will have low feelings of efficacy and worry a lot during the exam. That can be very distracting.

Self-efficacy and Your Thoughts, Motivation, Emotions, and Choices

In addition to the four sources of efficacy, it is important to understand how your efficacy influences you in your life. Bandura explained that efficacy influences aspects of our thinking, motivation, feelings, and the choices we make.[17] These are all part of your school experience. To make it clear how your sense of efficacy influences these four areas of your life, let's begin with the following familiar scenario: it is the beginning of the semester and you are choosing your classes. One of the classes is something you have never taken before – Psychology!

Thoughts

How does your sense of efficacy affect your thinking? For starters, it affects how you think about learning and school. Do you remember the first Psychological Key to Student Success? That's right, efficacy influences your beliefs about intelligence (mindset). Confidence influences the perception of your intelligence and whether it is fixed or changeable! It also influences how you set and pursue goals. Yes, that is PK2SS #3. If you have more efficacy, you are likely to set and pursue better goals, such as mastering what you study. If you lack confidence, you may think you aren't capable and, therefore, set lower goals and standards for yourself. Researchers have noted that if you believe you cannot attain a goal, you are more likely to reduce your pursuit of that goal. They hypothesized that this could be true for all achievement goal orientations.[18] If that is the case, it points to how very important your beliefs (PK2SS #1) are!

Efficacy also influences thoughts about the future. It is tough to imagine success in school if you lack efficacy in academics. If you have experienced a lot of previous academic success, however, you are more likely to feel confident in your abilities and predict future successes.

Motivation

Related to PK2SS #2, attributions, if you experience struggles in learning, high self-efficacy will make you resilient (able to bounce back) and tenacious (keep trying no matter what). However, low self-efficacy may lead you to give up. If you try hard but don't achieve at a high level, high self-efficacy can lead you to attribute the difficulties to lack of effort. In response, you will increase effort. However, in the same situation but with low self-efficacy, the attribution may be that you are not smart or capable enough. That may lead you to give up because you believe that you simply can't do it (regardless of effort). Students who have higher self-efficacy are more likely to "work harder, persist, and eventually achieve at higher levels."[19]

Suggestion #1: As explained above, having success experiences is the best way to build efficacy and increase motivation. In school, many of the things you need to accomplish are based on skills such as time management, goal-setting, and prioritizing. These are all skills that, once learned, make academic tasks easier, especially when you have many of them. Spend time learning about these skills and you will become more confident managing and successfully completing academic tasks.

Suggestion #2: One way to increase your motivation and your self-efficacy relates to PK2SS #3, goals. Setting proximal (smaller, short-term) goals with specific performance expectations (e.g., behaviors you will do) when you are first learning a topic or skill can enhance your motivation and self-efficacy.[20] As your skills and knowledge increase, setting more challenging goals will increase your motivation and self-efficacy. For example, when you first start learning a type of math, set a goal that you will complete two practice problems each night. As you get better at the problems, you can select more challenging problems to practice each night.

Suggestion #3: As you will see when you read about PK2SS #6, actively asking for feedback about how you are doing is an important skill. That's right. Asking for feedback and help is a skill. When you ask teachers for feedback, or when you seek clarification about feedback you already got from them, ask for specific ideas and advice. For example, tell them how you studied or how you went about researching and writing a paper. Getting feedback on the strategies you used has been shown to increase students' self-efficacy.[21]

Suggestion #4: You already learned that success experiences are the best way to increase efficacy, but you also learned that encouragement can be helpful too. Compliments and encouraging statements are great for increasing your motivation in the short-term. However, if you keep struggling or failing, they won't help much. Support and encouragement can increase your efficacy best when it relates to improving your performance through strategy suggestions.[22] Make sure you talk to your teachers about this. If they don't offer you specific ideas about what strategies you can use, ASK! Learning centers and tutors available at your school are great sources of suggestions as well.

Suggestion #5: Find teachers and peers who have studying and thinking habits that promote deep learning. Pay close attention to HOW YOUR TEACHERS THINK about topics and how they solve problems. Observe (and ask directly about) how successful friends and classmates tackle difficult assignments. How do they approach studying? Teachers and some of your peers can be excellent models from whom you can learn more effective studying and thinking strategies. This will promote your academic self-efficacy as you emulate (i.e., imitate) the effective strategies used by those people.[23]

Emotions

The third area affected by your efficacy is feelings. If you experience a great deal of self-doubt, how do you feel? Most feel worried. They are afraid of failure. They are afraid of looking stupid. They are afraid to even try so they avoid anything challenging. How can you succeed at the college level if you avoid challenges? Does that sound familiar? We talked about that when we considered the performance-avoidance goal orientation in PK2SS #3. Fear often lowers performance. So, in college, low self-efficacy can set you up to fail, not because you lack skill, but because you don't believe you can do it, feel afraid of failure, and therefore don't try (or don't try hard enough).

However, flip this over and look at the positive side. Higher self-efficacy leaves you feeling confident. When challenges arise, you don't feel fear. You feel motivated. You see an opportunity, not a threat. As a result, you dive in and set about achieving whatever it is that needs to be done. In that way, your feelings play a "major guiding and regulatory role in [your] cognitive and motivational systems."[24]

Suggestion: Learning to monitor and control emotions is something that is a challenge during adolescence but is a struggle that many experience into adulthood as well.[25] Taking care of yourself, tending to your mental health, and developing self-awareness will help you be a more effective and successful student. Basically this means you need to pay attention to your emotions, what leads to them, and how to effectively manage them. Emotions can be a great source of motivation. Reading this book is a step in the direction of self-awareness and, hence, better self-care!

Choices

The fourth area that self-efficacy influences is the choices you make. Think about the courses you choose. Not all of them are required; some are electives. You may choose them out of interest. Does ability ever factor into your decision? Do you look at the course requirements in the description and compare that with your perceived abilities? Confidence in your abilities will likely influence your choice of major and eventual career, not just elective classes.

Efficacy influences decisions to do or not do certain things in school. If you lack confidence in your abilities, you are less likely to try something. If you have high self-efficacy, you are more likely to take on a new challenge (i.e., set of courses, career path). Students with higher self-efficacy due to previous success are more likely to adopt approach goals.[26] The benefits of approach goals, compared to avoidance goals, were considered in PK2SS #3. Improving self-regulation (you will read about this in PK2SS #6) can increase confidence in abilities which, in turn, increases job attendance.[27] The same could be said about school. We know that attendance is linked to performance in school!

Final Thoughts

Confidence in school-related abilities is important to your level of achievement. It influences your thoughts, motivation, emotions, and choices. Because of the strong influence efficacy can have, it is worthwhile to consider it on your own. I suggest that you also discuss it with your teachers. They can probably help you build academic efficacy!

The next two PK2SS are all about self-reflection, self-control, and HOW TO THINK! So let's start by considering the fifth PK2SS. It has a crazy name. It is metacognition!

PK2SS #5 – METACOGNITION

In 1997 the American Psychological Association "highlighted metacognition as one of the more important factors in contributing towards effective learning."[1] That makes me curious. If it is so important, why do so few teachers talk about it? Have teachers ever mentioned it to you? Until now, have you ever even heard this term?

In 1979, a developmental psychologist named John Flavell coined the term "metacognition." He defined it as "thinking about thinking."[2] Metacognition is an awareness of your own thinking and how that can help you develop better learning strategies.[3] Part of being able to regulate your own learning is an "awareness of effective thinking and analyses of one's own thinking habits."[4] Metacognition also includes your ability "to appraise and manage the internal aspects of learning."[5]

Yes, I know. These academic-sounding quotations can be a bit much. Welcome to my world! Basically, metacognition is all about the awareness you have of your own thoughts and how helpful or hurtful your thoughts can be as you study, do homework, and complete exams. Awareness of your thoughts is critical to becoming a self-regulated learner (the next PK2SS we will consider).

Metacognitive Knowledge, Experiences, and Skills

In 2011, a professor named Anastasia Efklides from Aristotle University of Thessaloniki in Greece published an article that explained interesting details about metacognition. She suggested that metacognition is more than just an awareness of one's own thought processes. She asserted that metacognition is made up of three things: metacognitive knowledge, metacognitive experiences, and metacognitive skills.[6] I will highlight some of these concepts and how they will help you be more successful in college.

Metacognitive Knowledge – HOW to think

Metacognitive knowledge includes the awareness you have of your strengths and weaknesses as a learner and your beliefs about learning (PK2SS #1), your style of making attributions (PK2SS #2), and your goals (PK2SS #3). That means that I have been trying to build your metacognitive knowledge from the start of this book! Metacognitive knowledge includes what you know about how memory works and of different learning strategies and how to use them. It further includes your general level of self-awareness (something I'm trying to help you increase with this book). The purpose of metacognitive knowledge is to help you plan, strategize, and understand your studying efforts.[7]

Metacognitive Experiences – Your Feelings and Reactions

Metacognitive experiences include your awareness of a task and the processing of information related to it. For example, you are aware that you are reading this book right now, and you are trying to understand what it means and how it relates to your goals. Metacognitive experiences include the feelings of familiarity, knowing, and difficulty you experience when you are studying. For example, when you're reading something and think, "Hey, I've heard of that before," that is the feeling of familiarity. Similarly, as you are listening to a lecture and think, "Ya, I knew that already," that is the feeling of knowing. If you are studying something over and over and think, "I just don't get this stuff," that is the feeling of difficulty.

Metacognitive experiences are also related to your sense of confidence during a task (PK2SS #4). Your level of confidence will influence how easy or difficult learning feels. For example, thoughts such as, "I suck at this," might go with the feeling of difficulty whereas "So, this is what the teacher was talking about," might be a thought you have when reading the textbook is going smoothly.

Metacognitive Skills – Regulating Your Own Thinking

Metacognitive skills are strategies you use to control your thinking. These are not simple studying skills. Studying skills are tools. Metacognitive skills are thinking strategies that give you the ability to know how and when to use studying tools.

Dr. Efklides explained that our metacognitive experiences, such as a feeling that we are having difficulty understanding something, activate the metacognitive skills we use to regulate our thinking about the task.[8] Related to the section on metacognitive experiences, you can develop skills to control the thoughts you have when you experience the feeling of difficulty. Even something as simple as telling yourself, "Concentrate," is a metacognitive skill. Telling yourself that you 'must have missed a step and that mistakes are natural and ok' is a metacognitive skill. Telling yourself you did a 'good job' when you complete a task is a metacognitive skill. All such thinking skills are examples of self-regulation and are metacognitive skills. Successful students use "significantly more metacognitive monitoring and processing strategies" compared to less successful students.[9]

An Example: The Feeling of Difficulty

Sometimes studying does not go smoothly. Maybe you are taking a really tough class. As you work on the practice problems, you might struggle to figure out how to solve the darn problems. Maybe you think, "I don't get it. This is too hard," as you work on some chemistry problems or a paper for your English class. This awareness is a metacognitive experience called the feeling of difficulty. Everyone has these experiences...students, profs, parents, managers, lawyers, engineers, etc. This feeling occurs when processing of information is not easy.

Can you think of an example of a time when you experienced that feeling of difficulty? How did you feel? What did you do? How did it affect your motivation? The feeling of difficulty can be a good thing or a bad thing. It all depends on the attribution you make (remember PK2SS #2). An attribution is your explanation for why things happen. When you attribute the difficulty you're having to a lack of ability (i.e., "I'm stupid"), you are more likely to give up. If you attribute the difficulty to the task being hard or to a need to put forth more effort, you are more likely to keep trying.

The feeling of difficulty is one of the most important metacognitive experiences students have, and no one ever tells you about it. Teachers don't mention this when they talk about studying skills. This is probably because it is not the same as taking notes, highlighting, reviewing, or making flashcards, so it might not seem like an academic skill. But, the last time I checked, HOW YOU THINK is pretty relevant to your studying!! I have been trying hard to get this point across. How am I doing? Are you a believer yet? Remember, beliefs are PK2SS #1! ☺

Let's return to that crucial moment. Remember the situation:

You have experienced the feeling of difficulty and now you have to figure out the source of the problem, why the problem exists, and what you can do about it. If you believe that the level of difficulty of the task is responsible for your problem, you have to evaluate why it seems hard. Maybe you attribute the difficulty to the fact you are lacking information. That attribution is external and controllable. The problem (needing information) exists outside of you but is clearly something you can fix with a simple behavior or two. Maybe all you have to do is refer to your notes, check the syllabus, re-read the instructions, or jump online and look up an article. In this case, your motivation will be to look up what you need and then continue with the task. Often this is accompanied by a metacognitive experience called a 'feeling of confidence' that everything will get sorted out and you then anticipate success. That internal, metacognitive analysis happens almost automatically. It is part of the reason students don't pay much attention to their own thoughts...they are quick and seemingly automatic.

Let's look at another possibility. What do you think will happen if you believe the problem is, well, you? Maybe the quick and seemingly automatic analysis yields the thought, "I'm stupid." That attribution is internal, stable, and uncontrollable. As quickly as that attribution is made, feelings of frustration, anxiety, and defeat might follow. These attribution-dependent emotions create the motivation to avoid the source of the problem, which is actually your faulty attribution. Because you cannot crawl out of your own skin, and because you cannot instantly get smarter, you are motivated to avoid the task. For the moment, the frustration and anxiety may go away, but hours or days later the unfinished and difficult task is still lurking and the anxiety returns. That anxiety is sometimes called "fear of failure" and is more common for students with a performance avoidance goal orientation (PK2SS #3). The more you put things off, the more likely you are to make the failure come true. Let me say that again. The more you put things off, the more likely you are to actually create failure! How is your motivation for school now? What is really sad about this is that the "I'm stupid" attribution is usually WRONG. So, in effect, you imagine yourself into failure that was completely avoidable. Did I already mention that HOW YOU THINK is really important?

The Importance of Metacognition

People tend to have characteristic ways of thinking. Do you tend to give up or keep trying when something is hard? Maybe you put it off and justify your procrastination with, "I just need a little break." This is a crucial aspect of your thinking that will dramatically affect your studying, far more even than your actual knowledge or ability. HOW YOU THINK is very important. **All of the PK2SS we have considered so far are part of your metacognitive knowledge and can be used as metacognitive skills once you master them!** That's right. Everything you have learned about motivation, beliefs, attributions, achievement goals and interest, and self-efficacy are now part of your metacognitive knowledge. Soon, even the ideas about metacognition will be part of your metacognitive knowledge!

In 2002, Paul Pintrich made the argument that educators should teach metacognitive knowledge to students explicitly.[10] As you might have guessed, I agree. This book is designed to clearly point out the importance of beliefs, attributions, goals and interest, self-efficacy, metacognition, self-regulation, thinking errors and illusions, and culture and how they relate to your success as a student. They are the Psychological Keys to Student

Success! I am also trying to show how related concepts such as motivation, memory, emotion, and locus of control are related to your success. These psychological concepts go above and beyond simple studying strategies. I am trying hard to help you vastly improve your metacognitive knowledge and skills!

Without the personal and thinking skills I am talking about, studying and time management skills will only take you so far. Study strategies are weaker without increasing self-awareness first. The Dunning-Kruger effect (1999) says that if you lack a skill, you make mistakes and are also unaware of those mistakes.[11] Many students who lack metacognitive knowledge and skills don't realize it and, therefore, never figure out why their study strategies are not working. Let's talk about some specific aspects of metacognition that will make you a better student.

Kimberly Tanner's Article

Kimberly Tanner of the Department of Biology at San Francisco State University wrote an article about how teachers can help students become more aware of and effectively utilize metacognition in their studying.[12] Based on research, Tanner made a list of questions that students can ask themselves in order to become stronger in the metacognitive aspects of studying and learning. For example, before you study for an exam, you might ask yourself what studying and thinking strategies you can use to best study the material. You can ask yourself how much time you will need in order to master the information. As you study, you might ask yourself what information is most difficult and how you can seek clarification and assistance. After an exam, you might ask yourself how your incorrect answers compared with the correct answer. Were you close? Did you forget important details or did you have trouble with a more general concept?

Tanner's article is a treasure trove of great of questions you can ask yourself that will focus and guide your learning. These questions give you practice being more self-aware and intentional when it comes to learning. These questions can help you plan, monitor, and evaluate your learning. Before you attend a lecture or read a chapter in a book, ask yourself, "What do I already know about this topic?" This encourages you to analyze your own thoughts about a topic and, well, think about the topic. During a lecture ask yourself, what concepts are unclear? What is difficult? It is TOTALLY NORMAL and ok to be confused. Do not avoid it ... embrace confusion. As you're studying, write down questions you have and confusions you're experiencing. Those questions and confusions you are silently thinking about are examples of metacognitive experiences. This requires you to think about your understanding (or lack thereof). That is thinking about thinking!! In that moment, you are practicing metacognition. Good learning can come from it. I strongly urge you to look this article up and read it!

Metacognitive Skills for Homework – Suggestions

When you're working on homework, you can use metacognition to help you plan, monitor, and evaluate your work. For planning, ask yourself what material and resources you need in order to successfully meet the goals and expectations BEFORE you begin. Try to estimate how much time you'll need. Think about previous assignments you've done and how you might make this one better. While you're doing the assignment (DURING), keep track of how you're doing. Keep track of what strategies are working and which ones are not. Be aware of what is challenging and confusing. Ask yourself again about resources you could find and add that will clear up any confusion or difficulty you are having. Do you need to Google something or grab a dictionary? Should you find a resource in the textbook or your library's online databases? Maybe you should email the instructor and ask a question or two.

AFTER you have completed the homework, it is time to evaluate how you did. Compare the instructions, goals, and/or expectations given in the assignment with what you have produced. Here's a great suggestion: as best you can, pretend to be the instructor. What will the instructor like about your work? What can you anticipate will be the criticisms? Anticipating criticism is often related to the confusions you experienced, the sections you rushed through, the resources you did not use, things you chose to not look up or double-check, etc. If you 'know' something isn't very good, FIX IT!

Metacognitive Skills for Exams – Suggestions

Remember when we considered PK2SS #1, Beliefs and Mindset, I explained how your beliefs about the type of exam you're going to take will influence the way you study for it? A good metacognitive skill to develop is testing your beliefs! BEFORE an exam, think about all the different ways the instructor could ask questions, regardless of the type of exam. Think about how challenging he/she could make multiple choice exam questions. Always remind yourself that even what you think is an "easy" exam format could, in fact, be challenging. Further challenge your beliefs about exams by remembering what I'm about to tell you: a lot of college instructors like to use multiple choice questions that make you apply definitions and concepts even though they only teach you the definitions and concepts. Many don't teach you how to use/apply those terms and concepts first. So, a great metacognitive skill is forcing yourself to study all concepts like you will have to apply them. (By the way, if the prof gives examples in class, make sure you pay attention!)

Lev Vygotsky noted that young children will basically talk themselves through an activity. Yes, that's right. They talk to themselves, narrating what they are doing and why. If you have kids (or work with them), you have seen this. It is adorable! This is a concrete example of you being aware of your own thoughts. Yes, if young children can do it, you can too. Vygotsky called this "private speech" because it is talking that is meant only for you. Here's the tip: try this when you are working on a problem or trying to learn something difficult. Think out loud! This is NOT the same as simply reading aloud. I'm saying you should actually express your thoughts about what you are reading or working on. For example, "If I do this first, I can do that next," or "The prof said to do this but the text says something different. Which way is it?" By doing this, you are forcing yourself to be aware of your own thought processes. This is an example of a metacognitive skill.

Another great metacognitive exercise can be done AFTER an exam. Think about what strategies you used to study. Did you read and re-read the material? If so, how many times? Did you use flashcards? Did you re-write or summarize your notes? Did you highlight the book? Did you attend a study group? Did you test yourself? After you analyze the basic studying strategies you used, how much actual time did you spend studying? Now comes the interesting part. How did you do on the exam? How does your preparation compare to your results? Did your studying give you the results you wanted? Based on that analysis, now you have to think, "How will I study for the next exam?"

Gregory Schraw described what he called a 'strategy

evaluation matrix.'[13] It is a chart that lists cognitive and studying strategies you can use plus information about how, when, and why to use the strategy. You can make your own chart and create your own matrix! Make four columns: strategy, how to use, when to use, and why to use. Then make rows for all the different studying skills you use.

Here is an example that Schraw listed in his work. Consider "skimming" as a strategy. In the 'how to use column' he suggested that with this strategy you search for headings, highlighted words, and summaries. In the 'when to use column' he suggested that skimming be used prior to reading the chapter in detail. In the 'why to use' column he suggested that skimming gives you a conceptual overview and that it will help focus your attention.

As you fill in the details of your own chart, you will be identifying metacognitive and self-regulated learning (PK2SS #6 coming up next) strategies! This is an awesome exercise. For example, let's say you highlight passages in a textbook as you read. Once you list the strategy, you have to figure out how, when, and why you use the strategy. This requires that you examine your own thoughts about the strategy. THAT is an exercise in metacognition! Another strategy example is chunking. Do you re-read information? Do you make flashcards? What might you write in the how, when, and why columns? Make the chart!!

The Relationship between Metacognition and PK2SS #1, 2, & 4

Consider the relationship between your beliefs about yourself as a student (PK2SS #1 –Beliefs and Mindset) and metacognition. You came (or will come) to college with self-beliefs about your academic ability. These self-beliefs are part of your metacognitive knowledge. For example, how do you define yourself as a student? Are you a "good" student (by the way, what does that mean...what are the qualities)? Are you a "hard worker?" Are you "committed?" Are you "lazy?" Are you "just ok" or "good enough?" These ideas reflect your beliefs and mindset (PK2SS #1), your attributional style (PK2SS #2), and your self-efficacy (PK2SS #4). They influence your approach to school your approach to individual courses and assignments.

Let's say you believe you are a good student because you got As and Bs in high school. You are confident when you enter college, choose your classes, and work on assignments. What do you think will happen if you find that classes are harder than expected? What thoughts will you have as you work on something you don't understand? What feelings will you be aware of in that instant? Those thoughts and feelings are metacognitive experiences. Now imagine you arrive at college full of self-doubt (low self-efficacy). What thoughts and feelings will you have about classes and assignments? How will those thoughts and feelings affect your motivation and effort? This is another reason for understanding metacognition. It directly influences your motivation!

Metacognition affects your performance before, during, and after you do an assignment. As I just explained, you come to college with ideas about your ability before you do an assignment. These pre-existing ideas include thoughts about your abilities, knowledge base, skills, goals, and expectations for success. But this is general and will vary class to class and assignment to assignment. Once you are doing an assignment, you start having thoughts about your ability, skills, etc while you work on it. For example, if the assignment is really tough, you might start doubting your ability and skill. After the assignment is submitted and graded, a good result will bolster your confidence (PK2SS #4) and fuel positive thoughts and feelings about your skill and ability. However, negative feedback might shake your confidence. Do you see how metacognition works before, during, and after an assignment?

As college teachers, we want to help weaker students become more skilled and confident, and help the already-strong students be even more skilled. A really important part of our job is also evaluating whether your beliefs about your abilities are accurate or not. I have met a lot of students who got A's in high school and who, therefore, believed they were good students. But some of them lacked academic (e.g., reading and writing) and personal (e.g., work ethic and perseverance) skills that led to difficulties in college. Alternatively, I have met students who have had many negative and failure experiences in school prior to college who are actually very insightful, intelligent, and skilled.

Both cases are unfortunate. Students who believe they are more skilled than they really are experience surprise, anger, and frustration when they get negative feedback. As such, some do not believe that feedback, blame their instructors (i.e., make a bad attribution), and drop classes. Rather than trying to get better, they quit. On the other hand, students who are capable but don't believe in themselves may be afraid of failure and, in the face of any challenge, doubt themselves so much that they quit too. For college instructors, both types of students require attention. We have to try and maintain a high standard (college is referred to as "higher education" for a reason) while encouraging and motivating students to stick with it. We can't MAKE you change your thoughts. We need your help. Become aware of your metacognitive knowledge and metacognitive experiences, understand how they influence your motivation for and perception of college, and harness them and use them to your advantage. Self-monitoring is a difficult but important metacognitive skill for academic and personal success.

Metacognition and Your Feelings and Motivation

Dr. Efklides suggested that metacognition also helps us understand the link between feelings and academic motivation.[14] When we are working on a task, we may experience intrinsic motivation, the kind of motivation we get when we are really interested in something. This is usually accompanied by pleasant feelings. Together, that motivation and those pleasant feelings are a positive metacognitive experience. In this case, the result can be more task focus, increased desire to engage in and complete the task, and persistence. Conversely, if a task is perceived as boring or irrelevant to our goals, you may have to rely on extrinsic motivation (such as the hope for a high grade in the future) to get through the task. Feelings such as boredom, disinterest, apathy, and annoyance represent an unpleasant metacognitive experience. In this latter case, it is more likely you may think to yourself, “Why bother,” or “What’s the point?” Such thoughts can erode your motivation.

Think of an assignment you did recently. The first step is reading the instructions, right? As a teacher I can tell you that many students don’t do this carefully. So, they are screwing up before they even start! The second step happens pretty automatically. In the moment, you’re aware of it but you often don’t pay very close attention to it. That second step is when you have the thought “That’ll be easy,” or “What? I don’t get it.” Of course, there are other thoughts you could have. The point is that you compare the task with your own knowledge and skills.

The feelings that come from that comparison are a metacognitive experience. If the assignment triggers thoughts of related knowledge and previous experience, you may have the "feeling of familiarity" or even a "feeling of knowing." If you do know about the topic, or are really interested in it, reading and understanding the new material may seem easy. In psychology, we would say that you are experiencing high "perceptual fluency." That is a fancy term that means the processing of information is going smoothly for you. High perceptual fluency inspires confidence and motivation. Sometimes, however, the assignment will require you to think a little harder because there is no obvious match between the task and what you know. This increased cognitive effort on your part signals you to consider that the task may be complex, difficult, or new to you. For some, this stimulates curiosity. As you think more about the topic, you may come to feel that you really do have knowledge or experience that is relevant but hard to recall.

Final Thoughts

Metacognition is a type of 'advanced' thinking skill. It will help you use studying strategies and increase persistence when studying is hard.[15] Metacognition "is a necessary precursor to self-regulation."[16] Guess what? Self-regulated learning is the next Psychological Key to Student Success!

PK2SS #6 – SELF-REGULATED LEARNING

May I offer you and nice, freshly-baked chocolate chip cookie? Does that sound good? How about a radish? Which would you prefer? In 1998, researchers presented 67 university students (who had been fasting for three hours) with a stack of freshly baked chocolate chip cookies and a bowl of radishes.[1] Some of the students were instructed to eat two or three of the cookies but not the radishes. Other students were told to eat two or three of the radishes but none of the cookies. The experimenters left the room and secretly observed the students through a one-way mirror for five minutes. If you were in the radish group, would you cheat and eat a cookie or could you resist the temptation?

The experimenters observed that those who were instructed to eat only radishes had a hard time resisting the cookies, but they did successfully avoid the temptation. After five minutes, the experimenters returned and gave all the students problems to solve. The students did not know the problems were actually impossible (there was no solution)! What do you think happened next? The researchers discovered something very interesting. The students who had been allowed to eat the cookies persisted in trying to solve the problems, on average, for over 18 minutes. The students who had been instructed to eat the radishes but not the cookies gave up trying to solve the problems, on average, after only 8 minutes. It was as if using their "willpower" tired them out!

Self-control is a bit like a muscle. When we use self-control, the muscle gets tired (and it seems like temptation gets stronger). Please keep that in mind the next time you leave studying for the end of a long day. You're much more likely to "give in" and watch TV than you are to study for hours, despite your best intentions. With training, however, the more we use our self-control, the stronger it gets.

With the sixth Psychological Key to Student Success, my goal is to help you work out and strengthen your self-control muscles! Self-control is a necessary personal resource in order to succeed in college.[2] It is not your parents' or your professors' responsibility to remind you to read, study, and complete assignments.

I strongly recommend you re-read that last paragraph...twice. Ok, you should highlight it too. Now memorize it and text it to all your friends. Tweet it. Post it on Facebook. Get personalized license plates (SELFCTRL). Most importantly, go tell your parents and professors you understand that reading, studying, and completing assignments are YOUR RESPONSIBILITY. They'll be thrilled to know you get it! With this book, I am trying to help you meet this responsibility, meet it well, and meet it consistently.

Unfortunately, many high school teachers and college professors work very hard to impose structure and control over your schoolwork. This is a mistake.[3] They then compound this with an even bigger mistake: they don't teach you the skills you need to internalize the control over your schoolwork. That is, they do not show you HOW to control yourself. For example, high school students need to learn how to transfer homework assignments into personal goals, how to set aside study time, how to make sure they complete their goals, and how to anticipate the consequences for the decisions they make.[4] We live in a time when people have become very impulsive and impatient because we are used to high-speed internet and constant, ubiquitous (i.e., always presents) communication. Our patience, perseverence, and ability to delay gratification have been eroded. Understanding how to persevere and delay gratification are key metacognitive skills (PK2SS #5) which require self-control.

In general terms, "self-regulation" is the ability to control and direct your own behavior, thoughts, and emotions. In many ways, it is another term for "self-control." The next step up from simple self-control is self-regulated learning (SRL). SRL will help you control yourself better. It will also help build your academic self-efficacy and increase your thinking strategies and deeper learning.[5]

In a nutshell, self-regulated learning is about how you motivate yourself, set goals, focus your efforts toward achieving those goals, evaluate your performance, and learn from that process. It is a "dynamic process involving cognition, emotion, behavior, and context."[6] That means SRL involves the interaction between your thoughts, feelings, actions, and surroundings.

Many people have developed theories of SRL.[7] No matter what theory or bit of research you read, SRL deals with metacognitive skills such as planning, monitoring, and evaluating your work as well as cognitive strategies and studying skills like chunking, rehearsal, elaboration, and organization. SRL further includes metacognitive skills and motivational strategies such as modifying your beliefs, making better attributions, and managing your own emotions.[8] A person's "self-awareness and intention to act is what binds SRL and metacognition together.[9]

SRL is one of the Psychological Keys to Student Success because it mediates (i.e., helps explain) the relationship between you and your level of achievement.[10] Training students in the area of studying skills is only effective if it makes them aware of self-regulation strategies needed in specific learning situations.[11] In other words, you need SRL skills to make basic studying skills maximally effective. In addition, self regulation "forms an essential link between academic goals on the one hand and the quality of achievement behavior on the other."[12]

On the flip side, students who have the ability to do well are sometimes thought to be "underachievers," in part because of a lack of academic self-regulatory skills.[13] This helps explain why some really smart and capable students don't get good grades. They are academically strong but their lack of self-control leads them to not accomplish as much as they could.

What Are Self-regulated Learners Like?

Barry Zimmerman described self-regulated learners as students who actively seek out information, especially when something is unclear or confusing. They also accept more responsibility for their own achievement. He wrote that "they find a way to succeed."[14] Self-regulated learners understand the link between self-regulation and their level of academic achievement. They understand the importance of self-reflection, self-assessment, and self-improvement.

Dr. Zimmerman repeatedly stresses that self-regulated learners are proactive; they seek out opportunities to learn and they do it long before assignments are due and exams are looming. Self-regulated learners adapt to changing conditions and don't lose sight of their goals when challenges arise.[15] The benefits of learning the skills associated with self-regulated learning include greater motivation and achievement.[16] Research has shown that students with self-efficacy for self-regulated learning get better grades.[17] That combines PK2SS #4 with SRL.

Research also suggests that students with a mastery achievement goal orientation (PK2SS #3) are more successful in the area of SRL.[18]

Paul Pintrich's Model of SRL

Paul Pintrich was a leader in the area of self-regulated learning. He suggested that SRL occurs in four phases and explained that, in these four phases, you must regulate your thoughts, motivation, feelings, behavior, and the environment.[19,20]

Phase 1 is called 'forethought.' This occurs BEFORE the task. You think about and plan what you need to do (for example, a homework assignment). It includes the learning goals you have, what you might know already about the topic, and metacognitive knowledge (which, as you read previously, includes self-knowledge of your goal orientation and level of interest, your perceived level of self-efficacy, and your thoughts about how easy or difficult things will be).

Phase 2 is called monitoring. This occurs DURING the task. Monitoring includes your level of attention to and awareness of what you are doing. That means metacognition plays a key role. During the monitoring phase, you think about how easily you are handling the task. You are also aware of and are responding to metacognitive experiences such as the feeling of knowing or feeling of difficulty. These metacognitive experiences reflect the use of metacognitive skills like evaluating information and self-questioning that help you track progress toward your goal.[21] This helps you "discriminate between effective and ineffective performances."[22] Knowing when your studying is effective and when it is not allows you to modify your efforts.

During this phase you must also be aware of your level of motivation, feelings of efficacy (PK2SS #4), and the attributions (PK2SS #2) you are making, especially if you are experiencing the feeling of difficulty (PK2SS #5). Finally, monitoring includes practical issues such as time management and how much of an effort you are making.

Phase 3 is called control. Again, this occurs DURING the task. You actively respond to the thoughts, feelings, and motivations you noticed and experienced during the monitoring phase. Control is exerted on your attention, effort, motivation, use of studying strategies, and aspects of the environment. You employ studying strategies (such as note-taking, rereading, elaboration, memorizing, etc.), metacognitive skills (such as positive self-instruction), and environmental structuring (such as turning off your phone). You may also seek help directly from a teacher, teaching assistant, tutor, classmate, or friend.[23]

Phase 4 is called reaction and reflection. This happens AFTER the task has been completed. You consider how you believe you have done on the task. This includes your perception of your efforts and the attributions you make about your self-evaluated performance. I suggest that this phase includes the attributions you make when you receive formal feedback from your instructor about your performance.

Within Pintrich's framework, we can see all the Psychological Keys to Student Success operating!! Check this out:

- In the forethought phase, beliefs (PK2SS #1) about learning and your goal orientation (PK2SS #3) will affect your planning for the task you're working on.

- Confidence in your abilities (PK2SS #4) is relevant to all three time frames (before, during, and after) the task.
- During the task, metacognitive experiences (PK2SS #5) will help guide your effort and influence your attention and persistence.
- If you are experiencing difficulty during the task, you will generate explanations for this (PK2SS #2) which will reflect your beliefs (PK2SS #1) and LOC (part of PK2SS #2) which will, in turn, affect your motivation.
- After the task is done and you receive feedback, you will again have to explain your grade (PK2SS #2) and compare this outcome to your beliefs (PK2SS #1), your beliefs about your abilities (PK2SS #4), and perhaps (hopefully) recognize any thinking errors (PK2SS #7) you might have made.

Barry Zimmerman's Model of SRL

In an article he wrote in 1998, Dr. Zimmerman explained that self-regulated learning involves "self-generated thoughts, feelings, and actions for attaining academic goals."[24] Essentially, this means that students need to direct their own thinking, feelings, and behavior as they try to achieve in school. It doesn't matter how small or big your goal is (e.g., read a few pages before bed or study for weeks for a comprehensive final). You must control yourself in order to accomplish it.

Dr. Zimmerman suggested six psychological dimensions related to self-regulated learning that I will share, explain, and exemplify with you. The six dimensions are motivation, study strategies, time management, feedback, the environment, and other people.[25]

1. Motivation

This is the first dimension of Zimmerman's model of SRL and, as you'll recall, it is a chapter all by itself in the book you're reading! As a college student, finding the drive to do a lot of reading and homework is challenging. What do you do when you just don't feel like studying or are bored with it? How do you make yourself study?

Think of all the personal factors that determine your studying behavior. Interest? Confidence? Energy level? Health? Perceived benefit? Other obligations? You can think about motivation as including your desire to set a goal as well as a process of staying on task once you start pursuing that goal. That second part, staying on task, is called "motivational regulation." It can be defined as "thoughts, actions, or behaviors [that students use] to influence their choice, effort, or persistence for academic tasks."[26] Motivation is really about a willingness to keep working on something, especially in the face of distractions and challenges.

Recall that intrinsic motivation comes from our desire to learn and that extrinsic motivation often reflects our desire to obtain a reward. Finding your own internal desire (intrinsic motivation) for taking, attending, and working hard in classes is often superior to doing it because you "have to" (extrinsic motivation). But extrinsic motivators like wanting a good grade and a better job are ok too. Of course, you are right if you are thinking that some courses are boring. There are some you "have to" take for your program, whether you want to take them or not.

Students with intrinsic motivation will have an easier time with even the most boring classes. Interest (PK2SS #3) is something you can develop, even when you think you can't. Also consider that, in college, you will have many goals and certain goals will take priority over others at different times.[27]

What can you do about your motivation? This is a very big topic and there are no guaranteed quick fixes. As well, there are medical and psychological conditions that affect our levels of motivation. However, the average student benefits from educated advice about how to increase motivation.

Suggestion #1: Remember that SRL is about planning, monitoring, and evaluating work. Setting goals is part of the planning phase of SRL. They help you organize what is to be done, provide a source of motivation, and become the benchmark you use to evaluate your progress. As such, they are actually both a starting point and an end point.

Each and every day, I strongly recommend that you set goals for what school work you want to accomplish THAT day. This is like a to-do list. In my opinion, students sometimes have tunnel vision when they get advice from parents and high school counselors who urge them to think about the future. They try to think of what life will be like 5 to 10 years in the future and forget about the importance of short-term goals.

"Wait, Troy. Are you suggesting that I *not* think about my future?" NO! My answer is, however, that your future is like looking at a map before you take a long road trip. You see yourself at the starting point and you measure how far it is to the destination. If you focus only on that distance, the trip may seem like it will take forever and you might start feeling discouraged or frustrated. But, if you break that long road trip into smaller pieces (remember chunking), it feels much more manageable. For example, when I lived in Canada I often drove to Minneapolis,

Minnesota to visit family. The trip was only 350 miles but, after driving it a few times, it started to feel really long. Rather than focus on the 350 miles (or 325, 300, 275 miles left to go), I would simply focus on the next small town or scenic spot along the way. Suddenly, the long trip seemed like a series of short jaunts. That way, the trip seemed to whiz by quickly.

Getting through a semester, let alone getting all the way to graduation, can seem like a long time. So instead, focus on what you are going to accomplish TODAY. Research has shown a relationship between higher achievement and students who set specific, proximal goals compared to setting distal goals.[28] Remember that a proximal goal is short-term in nature and usually involves breaking a large task into a series of smaller tasks. You need to see that your current academic achievement is connected to the attainment of your future goals.[29] Other research has shown that long-term goals are great motivators to get you started in a certain direction but it is the short-term goals that help you focus your attention and stay on task (part of SRL).[30] Having these short-term goals also gives you information and feedback in the short-term which allows you to modify your strategies and make sure you are constantly on track for the longer-term goals.[31]

So, are you going to read part of a chapter? When? How many pages? Are you going to research information for that paper? Where are you going to look? How much time will you spend? Are you going to do some of those chemistry problems? When and how many? Set small goals EVERY day. If you do, you will be amazed at how much you accomplish over the long term.

<u>Suggestion #2</u>: Top athletes visualize the achievement of their goals. They mentally "see" themselves performing tasks well

before they physically practice skills and before they compete. You can do this too. I have met many students who talk constantly about all the reasons they can't do homework on time or study enough for tests. I can tell that they "see" their kids misbehaving, their jobs, their family obligations, etc. in their heads as they describe the obstacles to academic achievement and success. They fear poor grades and failure. They "what if" themselves into doing nothing. All of this is bad visualization. They are visualizing failure. Of course this makes school hard!

The good news is that you have a choice. Every moment, you can actively choose what you spend your time thinking about. Spend more time "seeing" yourself in the library reading after class instead of catching up on what are usually unimportant text messages (the "lol" and "wtf" and "how r u" can definitely wait). Imagine yourself sitting comfortably and working on your homework after work instead of "vegging" in front of the television. Imagine yourself saying no to people who make too many requests for your time. Imagine telling them that school is THAT important to you (real friends and helpful family members will respect that).

This kind of visualization (called a "process simulation") can be an effective SRL strategy that also can help change negative learning beliefs (remember that beliefs are PK2SS #1).[32] For example, one study showed that women completing their undergraduate degrees who imagined success performed more successfully than those who imagined failure.[33]

Researcher Monique Boekaerts said that motivational self-regulation is your effort "to produce favorable states of mind and positive outcomes, or prevent undesired events and unfavorable outcomes."[34] Included in motivational self-regulation are things like addressing your beliefs (PK2SS #1), modifying your attributions (PK2SS #2), considering your achievement goal orientation (PK2SS #3), planning (part of metacognitive skills in PK2SS #5), developing coping strategies to reduce stress, and accessing academic and social support. Look at all those Psychological Keys to Student Success that are part of motivational self-regulation!!

<u>Suggestion #3</u>: As you know, self-efficacy is the confidence you have in your ability to accomplish something (like achieving a goal) and it varies depending on the situation. For example, if you are like me, you have more confidence in your ability to learn things like history, sociology, and psychology than learn things like math and architectural drafting (I'd make some really screwed up buildings). In terms of school, what is your level of self-efficacy for studying effectively? Do you think you're a good studier? What is your level of self-efficacy in each one of your classes?

Look back at PK2SS #4 and review the sources of self-efficacy. You will see that the best way to build your studying and academic self-efficacy is to practice the skills until you are actually good at them. It is easy to be confident when you have EVIDENCE that you are good at something. This confidence will also link strategies you're good at right now to your motivation and the attributions you make.[35] In addition, self-efficacy can propel you to set more ambitious goals, persist in the face of difficulties, and engage in more SRL![36]

<u>Suggestion #4</u>: You can use behavioral principles to reinforce good studying behavior. This fits together with and is a positive example of extrinsic motivation. You can connect a treat or a break with the completion of a proximal goal. For example, you can promise yourself 10 minutes of texting AFTER you finish

reading ten pages in the textbook. You can also give yourself verbal rewards any time (e.g., "I'm doing a good job."). This relates to the use of positive self-talk and self-encouragement (e.g., "Only three more pages to go. Stick with it."). Encouragement, as you may recall, is a way to improve your self-efficacy. You don't need someone else to encourage you. You can encourage yourself! Positive self-talk is a metacognitive skill.

Suggestion #5: Each time you read or study or complete a homework assignment, remind yourself why this is important. Purposely think about why you enrolled in college in the first place. Make your homework and your studying a reflection of your chances at getting a good job. Imagine that your assignment for a class is going to be stapled to a job application! Take even one minute as you begin your schoolwork to reflect on this ultimate value. Notice how this relates to the visualizing I mentioned in suggestion #2!

Your belief that a topic is interesting and important to your future goals will guide your choice whether or not to be engaged and use good learning and study strategies.[37,38] Finding the value in a class as it relates to your future connects you to the class and information but that alone doesn't necessarily lead to good grades. Once you are connected to the importance, you have to use motivation strategies to actually achieve. But thinking about value is a good place to start.

Suggestion #6: Christopher Wolters offered an idea I like very much. He called it "interest enhancement."[39] Do whatever you can to increase your enjoyment of each academic activity. When you are studying, for example, quiz yourself (an extremely powerful studying and metacognitive skill) and give yourself points for correct answers. Pretend you're on a game show. When you earn a certain number of points, you win a treat or a break (see how this can connect to suggestion #5?). If you read about something interesting, Google it during one of your earned breaks and learn more about it. These are just a couple of examples. You can make up your own fun!

Please keep in mind that interest in a topic may require effort on your part. Your level of engagement influences your experience of interest (part of PK2SS #3) and that your efforts to self-regulate interest can affect goals and their outcomes.[40] It is not the instructor's responsibility to "make" you interested! The reality is that some teachers suck. Some classes really are boring. But if you sit there blaming everyone and everything else for your lack of interest (an example of a very unhealthy attribution), you will probably do poorly. Helplessness and blame are the opposites of SRL! They can trigger negative feelings that will distract you from your goals.[41] Developing interest is related to intrinsic motivation and a willingness to make greater effort.[42]

2. <u>Study Strategies</u>

This is the second dimension of Zimmerman's model of SRL. So, what study strategies do you have in your studying tool belt? How do you decide what strategy to use for your sociology exam? How about your English exam? What strategies do you have for studying how to do algebra problems?

Students must first be exposed to a variety of studying strategies. This happens through direct modeling and teaching as well as through some trial and error. Friends and classmates can sometimes give us good studying ideas too. The next thing is using and practicing the strategies. Studying strategies are like any other skill; they must be practiced before you will be good at them. Then you have to be able to select the appropriate (i.e., most effective and, perhaps, efficient) strategy for any given topic or task. Developing the ability to select a good strategy is part of self-regulated learning. Awareness of what studying strategy will be most effective is a key metacognitive skill. For example, just because someone says using flash cards is great does not mean it will work for you!

Dr. Zimmerman listed 14 self-regulated learning strategies. As you read this list, think about how many of these strategies have come up in our consideration of the Psychological Keys to Student Success. Here is Dr. Zimmerman's list: "self-evaluation, organization and transformation, goal setting and planning, information seeking, record keeping, self-monitoring, environmental structuring, giving self-consequences, rehearsing and memorizing, seeking social assistance, and reviewing."[43]

As noted in the discussion about self-efficacy, practice is the key. Learning strategies range from the simple (e.g., memorization) to the complex (e.g., understanding connections between topics that seem unrelated). Keep reading and learning about these strategies. Keep developing them through practice. If you do, your confidence, ability, and results will grow.

3. Time Management

This is the third dimension of Zimmerman's model of SRL. Self-regulated learning requires skills in organization and scheduling. Time management is really just organization related to time. Oh oh! Are you not-so-good at time management? In college, fewer people will provide you with extrinsic motivators like reminders. So, you need to do a little planning on your own. To be good at this, you need to develop not just planning skills, but also the ability to accurately assess and estimate how much time homework, assignments, and studying will take. You will read more about time and how to use it better when you read PK2SS #7.

Self-regulated learning is more time consuming than simple reading and memorizing strategies. SRL is all about planning, monitoring, and evaluating your efforts. It requires the use of metacognitive knowledge and skills. You have to budget more time for studying to accommodate these more advanced thinking skills. Keep this in mind! But also know that the time "cost" is offset by all the benefits of developing a mastery achievement goal orientation and the higher level of achievement associated with metacognitive skills and self-regulated learning.[44] With practice, metacognitive skills and self-regulated learning make your studying more efficient!

4. Feedback

Receiving and learning from feedback is the fourth dimension of Zimmerman's model of SRL. Have you ever gotten an assignment or exam back and thought, "HEEEEY?!?!" Did the comments seem mean or too critical? Well, sometimes they are because some professors...suck. I think this is the second time I said that in this chapter...lol. Most college profs don't suck, but they have very limited time. They only have one semester to prepare you for the next class or maybe even the next program or your career. They must communicate your strengths and weaknesses quickly. And don't forget it isn't just you in the class. Many are teaching hundreds of students each semester.

Instructors' comments should be considered, whether you like them or not, in order for you to learn. If you don't understand the feedback, GO ASK. This is like mining; sometimes you will not find the meaning in feedback if you don't dig a little! Please keep in mind that most students, compared to everything there is to know about a subject, do not know very much. That's why you are in school. So, as hard as this is to believe, your paper/exam may not have been as good as you thought it was! Students who are more successful see "failure" as an opportunity to learn, not as an attack on their character (remember PK2SS #2, attributions). Students who are more successful use the feedback to modify their strategies and efforts.

Suggestion #1: Understand that your success in college is about learning the material AND learning what your professors expect and want. This varies from class to class and professor to professor. I always tell my students that it is important to "read the audience." You must understand who you are talking to or, in your case, the professor with whom you are dealing. Research as suggested that "students' success in college depends not only upon their explicit understanding of course content but also their implicit understanding of how to demonstrate that knowledge in ways that will satisfy each professor's expectations."[45] I don't like the idea that you should try and figure out somewhat hidden (i.e., implicit) expectations. Rather than guess at the professor's expectations, GO ASK. Get feedback and more information about assignments, exams, and general expectations!

Suggestion #2: Look up the word "umbrage." Get going. Seriously. You have to look this one up. GO NOW! Did you find it? If that term applies to you, this is where you must begin. Reducing 'umbrageousness' is key. It is hard to learn from constructive criticism if you are umbrageous. Even if the instructor's feedback did not seem very nice, interpreting those comments as a personal attack will only make you ignore, dismiss, or argue against them. Please remember the importance of PK2SS #2, attributions. Considering the comments as suggestions about how to improve is a MUST.

Suggestion #3: This might sound nasty but, GET OVER YOURSELF. As a college student, you should expect to be imperfect. Getting 90-100% is (or should be) reserved for true excellence. It takes time, a lot of learning, a lot of screwing up, a lot of patience, and a lot of self-discipline to achieve excellence. Considering the feedback from someone who knows way more than you about a topic is a good first step. Remember, you submit assignments and exams for evaluation. When you get the evaluation, regardless of whether it matches your expectations (PK2SS #1), be grateful for the opportunity to learn from someone who is more educated and/or experienced. That perspective will serve you better than thinking the instructor as an idiot.

Suggestions #4: Students with a performance goal orientation (PK2SS #3) often only glance at the grade they receive. Many basically look at the grade and then discard the assignment.[46] However, especially for students who are somewhat uncertain about their abilities or who fear failure, feedback can point to strengths as well as offer useful suggestions about how to improve skills. This can help you feel more in control of your learning and grades.

In my experience, many students treat assignments like they are discrete, independent events that are over once they are handed in. It is like, once the assignment is done, it disappears from the students' minds. POOF! With that attitude, there would be no need to review the graded assignment and consider feedback. However, while any given assignment may be graded and done, there will likely be many more assignments that require you to use many of the same skills, such as understanding and following instructions, writing in a particular format, expressing complex relationships between topics, building an original idea, supporting and defending those ideas with research, comparing and contrasting a variety of viewpoints...the list goes on and on. Feedback from instructors can help you understand all of the above. Plus, as you get more feedback from different instructors, you will have more and more perspectives about how to complete assignments effectively. Given that you are paying for school, think of feedback as one of the important pieces of learning you are paying for! Feedback can be like learning gold (even when it stings).

5. The Environment

The environment is the fifth dimension of Zimmerman's model of SRL. No, he didn't mean deforestation or clean energy. This refers to WHERE you study. Earlier I joked about your kids terrorizing the dog. Is this an environment in which you want to study? Personally, I need silence to study well. But that's just me. The ultimate thing to concern yourself with is getting the results you want. If you are getting A's while studying in a construction zone or the middle of an amusement park, more power to you. But most students I meet are not getting A's, so does your studying environment need modification? Finding a place free from distractions is usually helpful. Research has shown that students who deal more effectively with their studying environment are more likely to succeed, even compared to students who have an equal amount of academic ability.[47]

Suggestion #1: I always recommend a quiet place to study. That is my bias. Dorms can be crazy. If you have kids, well, they can be crazy (lol). Trying to study at work, where there are a lot of interruptions can be tough. Students sometimes have to make do with what little time they have. So you may find yourself trying to study in these environments, and I respect your effort. But, whenever you have a choice, exercise the choice and find a quiet place. Can you stay longer (or arrive early) at school and use the library? If you are at home, will closing a door and putting earbuds in help (earbuds are nice in that they double as ear plugs...you don't have to have music on)? Can you walk to the park or the lake and sit on a bench and read?

When I was in school, I'd stay at the library until it closed. Then I'd use the tunnels to get to another building on campus and find an open classroom. I would stay there, alone, until I was finished accomplishing my goals for the day. I even used this suggestion while I wrote this book for you. I did some writing in a lawn chair on the shore of the lake near my home. At home, I keep things quiet. When I am at school, I close my office door. Yes, I take my own advice!!

Suggestion #2: It is important to consider not just external distractions like noise, but internal distractions as well. Things like depression, anxiety, relationship problems, drug and alcohol addiction, and bereavement don't just magically go away because it is time to study. They are HUGE internal distractions. Please do yourself an incredible act of kindness and find support and counseling. Talk to your doctor. Open up to your minister/pastor. Reach out to family members and friends. Do something to address these issues so they do not keep you from achieving your goals.

6. Other People

Dealing with other people is the sixth and final dimension of Zimmerman's model of SRL. "Wait, how is SELF-regulated learning about OTHERS? Ok, Troy, you were making some sense until right now." Let me explain.

Who you choose to study with is a very important decision you make (if you choose to work with others at all). Study groups can be very helpful. They can also be a disastrous waste of time. As well, students have the opportunity to choose certain professors, tutors, support staff, and other students as models and mentors. Choose carefully! The final way others are important to self-regulated learning has to do with whether or not you seek help. Some topics are confusing. Sometimes the instructions for assignments are not perfectly clear (much to the chagrin of the prof who wrote them). For that matter, an entire course can be brutal. Students who seek out their instructors, teaching assistants, and/or tutors are more likely to succeed than students who suffer in silence. Students are afraid to ask questions and for help because they don't want to look stupid (remember PK2SS # 1, 2, & 3). The only way you can be stupid is if you don't know AND you don't ask (you will read about this more in PK2SS #7).

Suggestion: An effective method of self-testing your knowledge is to evaluate others and be evaluated by others. For some, this works well when a group of classmates agrees to study together. Here is a cool exercise. As a group, write out to-be-studied material but purposely make some errors. Then exchange papers and see if you and your group members can spot the mistakes. More importantly, can you correct the errors without assistance (a true test of knowing)? Finding and correcting errors is a great way to learn.

Keith Topping found that students who participate in "peer assessment" activities get higher grades and have more positive attitudes toward learning. He also explained that this kind of activity creates a number of other benefits including more focused attention on the task and increased reflection on what students are studying (that is a metacognitive skill).[48] In my opinion, this serves another very important function: it helps people deal effectively and in a non-threatening way with mistakes. Many students are afraid of mistakes. They react very defensively to comments that point out errors. Dealing with mistakes in the manner described above demonstrates the usefulness of mistakes; making and correcting mistakes is a powerful studying and learning tool.

7. <u>Summary/General Suggestions</u>

I know I said there were six key parts in Zimmerman's model of SRL. Yes, I can count. The following list is a summary of information by two articles written by Dr. Zimmerman.[49,50] I thought you might use it as a type of checklist for your own behavior. If you see that you don't do some of these things, you might consider making them part of your goals for a course. Pick just one thing and try to incorporate it into what you do this week. Making a little change now is the start of a good new habit! For example, you can decide to ask one question in each class session you attend as a way to increase your participation (and interest).

- Arrive prepared for and participate in class. Express interest in the subject.

- Offer relevant information and ideas that were not in the text when you participate.
- Express and defend opinions that differ from that of classmates and the teacher.
- Ask insightful questions.
- Volunteer for special/extra tasks or activities (if there is that opportunity).
- Make lists of what you want to accomplish when you study.
- Schedule studying and homework time every day.
- Complete assignments on time or early.
- Check work carefully (proofread) before turning it in.
- Keep track of completed assignments and what still needs to be completed.
- Seek help from the teacher if you're having difficulties.
- Solicit information from the teacher about upcoming tests/exams.
- Ask for additional details about teachers' expectations for assignments.
- Ask for more information about feedback you receive from the teacher.
- Be aware of how you have done on a test before you get the results.

Final Thoughts

My hope is that you are having "AHA!" moments. All of the PK2SS are related and they all have to do with HOW YOU THINK. If you want to succeed in school (and in life), this is where you must focus your efforts. HOW YOU THINK goes with you everywhere. You can't avoid it. You cannot escape it. So, do something about it!

Please consider this quotation: “It is not just the learner’s cultural background, demographic characteristics, or personality that influence achievement and learning directly; nor are contextual characteristics of the classroom the only things that shape achievement; but it is the learner’s self-regulation of his or her cognition, motivation, and behavior that mediates these relationships.”[51] In my opinion, that quotation stresses that your level of achievement is a complex interaction of many variables and that your thinking, motivation, and behavior are the key to explaining how you do in school.

Now that you are totally convinced that HOW you think is the key to your success, let’s consider some common thinking errors. Understanding thinking errors is PK2SS #7.

PK2SS #7 – THINKING ERRORS

A lot of the information we have considered requires you to develop self-awareness. Confucius, the Chinese philosopher who lived in a time 500 years before Christ, is known to have suggested that real knowledge is about knowing the extent of your own ignorance. LOL! That's encouraging. So, you're smart when you know how little you know? Yup, that's the idea!

The 7th Psychological Key to Student Success is about understanding common thinking errors people make. By knowing these common errors, you can take steps to reduce them and become a more successful student. There is a lot of psychological research that shows a disturbing trend: we think we know more than we actually do. Here are a few examples:

- Teenage boys rated their knowledge about how to use condoms as much higher than their actual knowledge of condom use.[1]

- Surgical residents' ratings of their surgical skills did not match their performance on standard board exams of surgical knowledge.[2]

- Students who do not achieve well and students who lack reading skills fail to know when they have accurately understood a reading.[3]

- College students who reported feeling 100% confidence in their answers were only 80% correct.[4]

Those examples make it clear why it is important to accurately assess your own knowledge and skills. Overestimation of your abilities can lead you to underestimate your learning and studying needs. One practical example of this is that overconfidence in what you know can lead you to not plan enough studying time. The result can be studying less and, therefore, achieving at a lower level than you wanted and expected.

"Hey, is Troy being mean to us now? What, he thinks we are stupid?!?!" No, I'm not being mean and I do not think you are stupid. Some students are very skilled. Some students are very unskilled. Most students fall somewhere in between. Anyone can overestimate how good he/she is at being a student. Becoming more self-aware and improving metacognitive skills (PK2SS #5) are important because "to the degree that people judge themselves accurately, they make decisions, big and small that lead to better lives."[5]

The Dunning-Kruger Effect

Justin Kruger and David Dunning stated that "when people are incompetent in the strategies they adopt to achieve success and satisfaction, they suffer a dual burden: not only do they reach erroneous conclusions and make unfortunate choices, but their incompetence robs them of the ability to realize it."[6] Basically this means that you don't know something, you make mistakes, and don't realize you are making the mistakes.

Let me give you a very common example. I also want to apologize in advance because, for some of you, this is going to sting. Many people say things like, "I seen him yesterday," and "She seen that movie before." Saying "I seen" is NEVER correct.

Why do so many people make that mistake? Many simply don't know it is wrong. They don't recognize the error and they are rarely (if ever) corrected. Therefore, they continue to make the mistake, don't realize it, and think it is totally ok. When they hear others say it, the same thing is true; they don't know it is a mistake and, therefore, think everything is fine. That makes them unable to accurately judge their own use of the word or others' use of the word.

If they do get corrective feedback about their mistake, they may have trouble believing it. That makes the feedback ineffective in terms of helping them learn from their poor performance.[7] They may actually believe that "I seen" is correct, making it harder to accept evidence to the contrary. Learning is hard when you think you don't have anything to learn!

Another example (noted in PK2SS #1) comes from studying skills research. In one study, only 11% of undergraduates practiced recalling information (i.e., self-testing) in preparation for a test, suggesting that 89% did not know about the benefits of self-testing.[8] If you don't know about a strategy, you don't use it and don't realize that you're making a mistake by not using it. This is one reason why learning a variety of studying skills is important. Also remember that studying skills are more useful if metacognitive skills (PK2SS #5) and SRL skills (PK2SS #6) are developed.

What Dunning and Kruger have studied and suggested is that the skills that make us good at something are the same skills we need in order to evaluate if we (or others) are, in fact, good at it. Therefore, if you lack effective studying skills, it will be difficult to effectively evaluate your studying skills. This is also true with respect to your ability to predict exam performance.

In a study of 141 psychology students, researchers had participants estimate how they had just done on an exam.

Students who performed the worst on the exam were the students who most overestimated their performance. They overestimated their performance by approximately 30%.[9] That is the equivalent of three letter grades! Unfortunately, this tendency to grossly overestimate performance persists for these weaker students even in the face of continuous negative feedback on exams.[10] They key to breaking this pattern is to make sure you ask about your poor performance and try hard to learn more and better studying skills.

In another study, when students were asked to predict which questions they got right and wrong on an exam, weaker students were less able to accurately predict exactly what they got correct and incorrect.[11] Another related problem occurs for people who suffer from the Dunning-Kruger effect: they are more likely to believe their error is in fact correct and, as a result, they believe that people who actually have the right answer are wrong.[12] Add to this another interesting research finding; the more times we recall information, the more confident we are that it is correct, even if the information we recall repeatedly is wrong![13]

A 2001 research study found that first year students' beliefs (PK2SS #1) about their academic skills did not match well with the evaluations they received from their instructors.[14] A survey completed in the 1970s showed that 70% of high school seniors estimated they had "above average" leadership abilities.[15] How can 70% of students be in the top 50% (average) of anything? That is statistically impossible! The mismatch between beliefs about our own skills and how we are evaluated is common and occurs in many professions, not just with students.

For these reasons I strongly encourage students to talk to their professors. You need to learn HOW successful students study, read, write, and take notes. Overestimating your ability can also undermine your motivation to learn. When it comes to self-regulated learning (PK2SS #6), why would you bother to focus and work harder if you don't think you have anything to learn?[16] Why would you bother to consider feedback from your instructors if you believe you are more skilled than you are? The monitoring and evaluating that is essential to SRL will be reduced by such ignorance.

Suggestion: Do not feel bad. Everyone is ignorant (by the way, ignorance simply means you don't know something). Compared to what we know, there is a ton of information out there we don't know. Even when you feel like you know something really well, assume that there is much more to it that you don't know. If you are completely certain of your knowledge, realize that there are connections between what you know and other things you don't. So, there's always more to learn. Stay curious!

Here is an example. Pretend that you are studying physics and learn Newton's third law. This law says that every action has an equal and opposite reaction. You read about this and understand all the examples in your physics text and from the lectures by your professor. On the exam you get the questions correct. So, you know it, right? Maybe you really do. But think about this: the next time you are upset and yell at someone and that person stops talking to you, could that be a relationship example of Newton's third law? Maybe not talking to you is an 'equal and opposite reaction' to your yelling? If we just think in terms of physics, that relationship example would never come to mind. However, there are always new and different perspectives to learn!

Errors of Omission

We are only aware of possible solutions to a problem that we can bring to mind. We can't think of the possible solutions we don't know about. That's the idea behind errors of omission. The solution we come up with is great if it works, but there might be a lot of other solutions we didn't come up with.

Why does this matter? Here is a research example. When people were asked to estimate how they did solving a Boggle puzzle, they rated their performance based on how many words they found, not how many words they might have missed. People also did not accurately judge how many words they missed.[17] Another good example comes from research that asked participants to find as many words as they could in the letters that make up the word "spontaneous." How do you think you would do? Let's say you get 100. That sounds pretty good, right? Well, there are more than 1,300 English words that can be made from those letters.[18] This is an example of how we overestimate what we know, how this overestimation leads to false feelings of confidence in our abilities, and how much we miss and really don't know. For example, in school, you might think that 80% correct on a test is pretty good. But what information was in the 20% you missed? Do you want your surgeon missing 20%? How about your lawyer, accountant, or the contractor building your house?

There is some very good news that comes from this idea about errors of omission. When you make people aware of their errors of omission, they become more accurate in the self-assessment of their performance.[19] For students, this is a crucial element of learning. Seeking out and paying close attention to feedback from teachers can greatly enhance not just your actual knowledge, but also your awareness of that knowledge. This is very true of studying skills as well. You can't use more effective studying strategies if you don't know they exist!

This book is designed to give you a lot of information and feedback about things you didn't know and didn't consider so that you can stop making a lot of psychological errors of omission!!

Tendency to "Self-enhance"

Some courses in school and topics in life are pretty clear-cut. Two plus two equals four. Water makes you wet (and sustains your life). But, in many other areas, the "right" answer is not so straight-forward. This is the case in psychology pretty much all the time. Dealing with thoughts, emotions, and social situations can be very complex; there are many perspectives and potentially correct answers. When situations and personal characteristics are unclear, we tend to "self-enhance" according to some research.[20] For example, people are more likely to rate themselves as higher than average on a personal quality like "being considerate" (that can be interpreted many ways) than on a quality that is easier to measure such as punctuality.

Below are three ideas from social psychology about the ways we tend to self-enhance. We looked at two of them when we considered attributions.

First, there is the self-serving bias. The key to understanding this bias lies in your understanding of PK2SS #2, attributions. Remember that the self-serving bias says you are more likely to attribute your successes to personal qualities like intelligence and ability but attribute your failures to external factors such as an unfair situation. As well, research shows that if we are skilled in some area (e.g., math, writing, fixing the car, etc.), we tend to believe that area is more strongly related to intelligence than areas where we lack skill.[21]

Second, there is the fundamental attribution error. When we see bad things being done by (or happening to) other people, we tend to attribute their behavior to their internal qualities. For example, when someone cuts you off while you're driving home and you say, "What a moron," you are attributing the driver's behavior to the driver's character and not considering the situation. Always consider the importance of the situation.

Third is the confirmation bias. This is a person's tendency to look for information that "proves" his/her belief to be correct. Face it, we like to be right, especially when dealing with our deeply held beliefs. If you believe that you are smart, you will look for "evidence" that you are smart. You will point out and remember things you did that are "smart." If you believe that someone is mean, you will look for and point out "evidence" that the person is mean. This tendency to try and prove ourselves right can help us all better understand why we sometimes cling strongly to ideas that are wrong. It also can help us understand why people who really doubt themselves find it hard to accept compliments.

Another contributor to inaccurate self-assessments of ability occurs when we focus on our own abilities and fail to consider the ability of others. Pretend that someone asks you, compared to other students, how good you are at finding your way around campus. Chances are, and research has shown, that you will probably rate yourself as above average. You make this rating on the basis that you have no problem getting around campus, totally ignoring the fact that most other students also have no problem getting around campus.[22] Similarly, if I asked you to judge your ability to get an A in an advanced astrophysics course, you'd likely rate your ability as lower than others, missing the fact that others are also not likely to be strong in astrophysics.

Hindsight

Have you ever struggled with a math problem and, before you finished it, looked up the answer in the back of the book? When you saw the answer, did you suddenly feel like the answer was obvious? "Oh! I knew that!" Well, I have a tough question for you: if you really knew it, why couldn't you figure it out on your own? Have you ever been reviewing an exam you got back, where the correct answers are provided for items you got wrong and exclaimed, "I knew that! Why did I pick that other answer?" I know why. You did NOT know the answer, no matter what you say about it after the fact. If you knew it, you would have gotten it right the first time! This tendency to say we knew the right answer after it is given to us is called the hindsight bias.

Suggestion: Remember the importance of self-testing? When you are working on a problem or when you are struggling to remember a detail you studied, looking up the answer and recognizing it does NOT constitute learning. The important question you should be asking is why you didn't remember the information without looking it up. This is a key metacognitive skill. Only when you can correctly recall it without help has true learning occurred. So, beware of the hindsight bias. Always test yourself!

Time

There is a tendency for people to underestimate how much time they need to complete a task, in part because we also tend to overestimate our ability to get things done. This is called the planning fallacy. We may focus too narrowly on the task at hand and ignore or discount the probability of other reasonably predictable events getting in the way.[23] This is especially relevant to today's college student who has a host of other obligations (i.e., jobs, kids, family, commuting, etc.) competing for a fixed amount of time.

Research has suggested, and I completely agree, that people need to focus more attention on the possible circumstances that may arise and plan accordingly.[24] Planning simply based on "I have 5 math problems that should take a half hour" is a very perfect world scenario based on no interruptions and no difficulties. Unfortunately, we don't live in a perfect world. That means an old saying is good advice: plan for the worst and hope for the best. It is better to plan more time and have extra if you finish early than it is to plan a set amount of time and run out before you complete what you needed to do. Part of the problem occurs when you write "do assignment" or "study for exam" in your schedule. These statements are ambiguous. Those scheduled activities give no indication of how much there is to know or how hard that information will be to learn.

Suggestion #1: A great strategy that will keep you in-tune with what you need to study for exams is to make a list of terms, names, dates, textbook pages covered, theories, etc. at the end of every class session. If you do this every day you will quickly begin to see how much you cover in a class before each exam and, therefore, how much time it will really take for you to learn ALL that information. Reviewing like this at the end of each class will also help you think about and remember the information in the first place!

The "discrepancy-reduction model" attempts to explain why

and how students use their studying time. It suggests that you first try to figure out what you need to do and how you will do it. Once that is sorted out, you will choose a studying strategy for the material that must be studied. Finally, you will monitor (PK2SS #5 & 6) how well you are learning the material. If the material has been learned, then studying can be reduced or terminated. If not, more studying needs to be done.[25] Does this seem like what you do? Well, it actually depends on what your studying goals are. If you are out of time, you won't be able to study more. If you are running out of time, you might actually choose to reinforce your understanding of the easy material. However, when the goal is mastery, students are more likely to study the material they judge is difficult first and longer.[26]

Your choice of what to study is not guided by the perceived difficulty of the material alone. There are many factors that influence your studying including how much time you have. Lisa Son and Janet Metcalfe from Columbia University did three experiments in 2000 and found that when students feel they are under a lot of time pressure, they are more likely to study material they judge as easier.[27] The implication for you is clear: if you don't have much time, you will study the easiest material before an exam; but if the difficult material is on the exam, you have a serious problem.

<u>Suggestion #2</u>: There was a neat study done in 2002 that looked at students' confidence in their ability to accomplish a task. The students were asked to rate how much time they thought they would need to complete a task. They were asked to estimate how much time they needed to do the task so they were only 50% sure they'd get it done in time. They were also asked to estimate how much (more) time they would need to complete the task so they

were 99% sure they'd get it done in time. You would think that the 99% rating would be pretty good and that most would actually get the task done in time. NOPE! Only 45% of them got the task done despite being 99% sure they would.[28]

Given that college is supposed to be a challenging experience designed to prepare you for harder classes and eventually a career, you should expect to encounter difficult material on exams. The solution lies in making sure you have enough time to study. If you have many other responsibilities, this will be hard. You cannot create time (in a literal sense). You must plan ahead and start studying many days, even weeks before an exam in order to effectively deal with difficult material.

<u>Suggestion #3</u>: From this, you can learn and adopt a simple weekly strategy. On Sunday night, look at your schedule for the coming week. You see what you have planned. Now try to anticipate likely delays and the needs of other people. Check the weather. Are there birthdays? Is someone ill? No one expects you to be able to forecast everything but you can do a little thinking ahead and build in some time buffers for your most important obligations and task deadlines.

Previous research stated "it is a problem when people concentrate [on what they have to do] and ignore the knowable fact that background circumstances from everyday life often sneak in to interfere with one's plans."[29] Basically that means we can get so focused on what we need to get done, we fail to anticipate likely problems that may come up. The research also noted that when Microsoft is developing software, it builds in an extra 30% more time to the development schedule over and above the estimated project completion time. If that kind of planning strategy is good enough for one of the most successful companies in the world, it should be good enough for you to at least try!

Honest Feedback

ALWAYS ask for feedback. It doesn't matter if you fail an assignment or if you get 100%. Well, it does; read the comments and consider them carefully. When you get feedback, if the comments are hard to understand or are unclear, go and talk to the instructor. Most importantly, if there are few or no comments to help explain your (good or bad) grade, you must go ask! A significant opportunity to learn is lost when you don't know what you did wrong or what you could do to improve.

Suggestion #1: Remember the Dunning-Kruger effect? The best way to address it is to get honest feedback about what you are doing wrong, where your skills are weak or lacking, and what you can improve. Remember errors of omission? To avoid them, ask instructors specifically what you may have missed or what you could have added that you didn't think of. Ask them what they would add to your assignment if they were doing it, not just grading it. And here is an interesting connection with PK2SS #1: when you ask for feedback, make sure you ask for advice on strategies, effort, and other things you can control. Such feedback can help you develop a growth mindset.[30]

If we look "at the types of feedback people get – or, fail to get – one often sees that the feedback people receive tends to be...insufficient to guide them."[31] Teachers are human and, like you, they are very busy. Some teachers are afraid to hurt other people's feelings. Many are uncomfortable with criticism, conflict, and confrontation themselves, so they avoid these things at all costs. If your instructors have these fears, they may not tell you the whole truth when they give feedback. You might think, "Ya, but teachers are supposed to be professionals who shouldn't be sugar-coating the feedback they give to students." You're right. They shouldn't. Sadly, some still do. Many believe that negative feedback will hurt your self-esteem. Research shows, however, it is more important that you get accurate feedback about what you can and cannot do.[32]

Holly Hassel and Jessica Lourey noted that instructors are also afraid of negative evaluations from students because those evaluations can impact instructors' job security (this is sad but sometimes true). So, instructors try to keep students happy. That means they might inflate your grade and might not tell you the whole truth about your performance.[33] This, unfortunately, is a vicious and self-fulfilling cycle of stupidity that will get in your way.

Suggestion #2: Don't let this happen. Go and ask your instructors specifically for honest and more detailed feedback. When you talk to them, express that it is important to your learning that you get the whole, unadulterated truth. Let them know you can handle some constructive criticism because the rockin', long-haired psychology prof who wrote this awesome book said it was ok!

Final Thoughts

You are doing a great job and are on the home stretch! Let's look now at the final Psychological Key to Student Success. It is time to consider how the first seven PK2SS do not apply to everyone in the same way. Culture, the eighth PK2SS, is a major contributing factor to our perspectives on all the PK2SS we have considered so far.

PK2SS #8 – CULTURE

Let's begin this PK2SS by considering a classic research study. American and Japanese university students were shown animated scenes of fish swimming. The fish were in the foreground and were more prominent than what was in the background (e.g., plants and smaller creatures). When tested, the Japanese students remembered more of the *background* information and the relationships between items in the scene compared to what American students recalled.[1] What factors might help explain this result, and how is this related to our consideration of successful students?

Up to this point, most of what we have considered has been based on Western theories, beliefs, values, and research. In fact, it is fair to say that much of the traditional research on academic achievement was badly biased from a Western point-of-view. "Western models of achievement motivation have at times been criticized as being culturally entrenched in an ideology of individualism."[2] But now more than ever, colleges and universities have a richly diverse student body. Within that diversity are students with markedly different upbringings, heritages, and customs. And please understand that cultural differences are not based solely on nationality. Diversity exists in socioeconomic status and whether you are a first-, second-, or later-generation college student.[3] As you can imagine, this has a significant impact on all the PK2SS. As such, this eighth and final PK2SS, the influence of culture, brings us full circle.

Researchers have tried to redress this limitation in cultural perspective, especially since the late 1970s. Sharper focus on the relationship between culture and academic achievement has become increasingly relevant. I cannot fully account for all of the research on culture's influence on all aspects of achievement motivation and academic performance in this chapter. However, I do want to introduce you to some of the main ideas. This will allow you to more fully appreciate the many ways people understand success and approach college. These people are not in college somewhere else; they are sitting right beside you.

When you read the information in this Psychological Key to Student Success, I would like you to keep the following definition of culture in mind. "Culture is the behaviors, ideas, attitudes, values and traditions shared by a group of people and transmitted from one generation to the next."[4] The values and traditions shared by the group allow it to "meet basic needs of survival, pursue happiness and well-being, and derive meaning from life."[5]

Based on that definition, and considering your own cultural background, how does attending school help you survive, pursue happiness, and derive meaning from life? Aren't you looking to improve your life by going to college? What do you believe about college and its purpose? What is the meaning of education? What does it mean to be educated and intelligent? I hope that you are recognizing that all of these questions address your beliefs, the first PK2SS. Like I said, we are coming full circle!

Before you continue reading about this PK2SS, I want to offer you this caution (and opportunity): many people are extremely sensitive about culture and race. Some are even "umbrageous." (You should have looked that up already. It means "easily offended.") They very quickly jump to conclusions. What you are about to read is simply a report about what <u>some</u> research in psychology has shown over many years, and about the need to increase our understanding, tolerance, and appreciation for the differences that exist. It is NOT about stereotyping. This PK2SS offers you an opportunity to examine your beliefs and attributions (PK2SS #1 & 2), increase your understanding and perspective, and become a better student.

Culture and PK2SS #1 –Beliefs and Mindset

How have your beliefs, values, attitudes, goals, and behaviors been shaped by your culture and how does that relate to performance in school? Culture shapes how you perceive people and situations, and even something as fundamental as how you organize your thoughts and knowledge.[6]

One of the most fundamental cultural distinctions made in sociology and psychology is the difference between cultures that are "individualistic" and those that are "collectivist." Individualistic cultures emphasize the uniqueness of the individual and how each person tries to develop his/her own talents and pursue personal fulfillment – achievement is a personal goal related to feeling good about oneself. Collectivist cultures emphasize the importance of the group and family and how each person contributes to the betterment of the group – achievement is not a reflection of one's individual interests and talents as much as it reflects a deep connection with and sense of obligation to the group and family. Said another way, individualistic cultures value independence; collectivist cultures value interdependence. The meanings of achievement, effort, success, failure, and autonomy vary considerably depending on culture.[7]

Another difference you find across cultures is the definition of what it means to be intelligent. What do you believe it is to be intelligent? In individualistic cultures (such as those in the United States, Canada, Western Europe, and Australia), intelligence is something that resides inside the individual; "whether the right stuff is DNA, genes, neurons, hormones, traits, abilities, motivation, drive, or talent, it is what is inside that counts."[8] However, other cultures around the world view intelligence differently:

a) Japanese culture values sociability, leadership, sympathy, social modesty, and have control over one's inner state as aspects of intelligent thought;
b) Indian culture values the connection between intelligence and morality and respect for elders, parents, and guests;
c) Chinese culture values the social and hierarchical nature of knowledge; respect for those who are more knowledgeable;
d) Ugandan cultures values intelligence as slow, deliberate, and helpful to others;
e) Puerto Rican culture values harmony within the group, as well as respect, obedience, and conformity.[9]

Imagine for a moment how these very different perspectives on intelligence would influence how the teachings in school are received and understood. For example, in psychology (and in this book so far), we have a strong bias toward the self. We talk about self-concept, self-esteem, self-efficacy, and self-actualization. Our entire perspective, historically in Western psychology, is based on the individual. Some of these teachings fly completely in the face of the perspectives of many other people around the world. In that way, for people from other cultures, learning Western psychology might be a little like trying to learn a whole new language. And, sadly, our teachings don't always do a good job respecting these different cultural perspectives. That is part of what I am trying to help everyone do with this eighth PK2SS –

respect the rich diversity in perspectives that exist when we consider what it means to be a successful student (and person), not just a success by typical, Western college standards. There is much more to intelligence, achievement, and happiness than your GPA and how much money you eventually make.

You don't have to travel around the world to find marked cultural differences in beliefs and the effects those differences have. For example, Fordham and Ogbu's seminal paper about the negative impact on African Americans of centuries of gross maltreatment included consideration of how this history has played out in achievement settings.[10] They noted that some African American students in Washington DC (in the 1980s) associated academic achievement with "white" behavior and, through something called oppositional identity, "were resistant to studying hard and getting good grades"[11] because "mastering academic work [was seen] as a one-way acculturation."[12]

This belief can easily be understood as a natural reaction to a long history of being discriminated against by the majority group. However, it is extremely important to note that most African American students want to get good grades, work hard, and achieve success in school and life. Many African American students only protested and rejected stereotypical White attitudes about success and education (e.g., having to speak 'properly,' taking certain 'hard' classes, and having mainly white friends).[13] Other research has clearly established that some minority students use the history of inequalities as a source of motivation and resilience.[14] They achieve at high levels and work to effect positive changes.[15] Others have gone as far to suggest that simply thinking in terms of "oppositional identity" inadvertently reinforces the stereotypes that African Americans do not value education.[16]

This type of resistance is not unique to African Americans. White Americans from lower socioeconomic backgrounds have been shown to resist school and achievement as well.[17] In fact, the argument can be made that any expectation for lower performance, regardless of your culture, can set up a self-fulfilling pattern of underachievement.[18]

Culture and PK2SS #2 – Attributions

When successful at accomplishing a goal, Westerners tend to take credit by attributing success to internal factors such as effort and intelligence. Such attributions bolster self-esteem and self-efficacy. When we are unsuccessful at accomplishing a goal, we often attribute failures to external factors such as unfavorable circumstances. Those attributions protect our self-esteem and efficacy and they preserve motivation for future tasks.

These attributions are not common across cultures. People from collectivist cultures are more likely to make external attributions for success and make internal attributions for failures. That is, they may give credit to the group for success and accept personal responsibility for failures. They are motivated by humility and social harmony. This pattern, one opposite to the Western pattern, preserves their motivation for future tasks.[19] In achievement settings, people from Eastern cultures appear to appreciate self-effacement (i.e., not drawing attention to yourself) compared to self-enhancement.[20] It is important to point out that people from collectivist cultures neither deny the importance of individual characteristics nor fail to take credit for individual achievement. They simply value social and situational attributions over personal ones.[21] Notice how 'opposite' these perspectives are. You find that people from other cultures are just as motivated to achieve and avoid failure; they simply come at it from a different perspective.

The existence of stereotypes and negative attitudes about different groups of people can have a significant impact on the attributions we make. A lot of research has been done on something called "stereotype threat." The idea here is that when a negative stereotype exists about a group of people, those people may come to fear that their behavior could in some way confirm the stereotype. *Hypothetically and simply for example*, if a majority of people believe that everyone who is "fat" is stupid, people who are overweight may begin to worry that if they do poorly in school it could "prove" the idea they are stupid. This can have a major and negative impact on their performance in situations where they are going to be evaluated, even if they do not believe the stereotype.

This is exactly what has been demonstrated to happen for many African American students. Sadly and incorrectly, there is a long history in the United States of people believing that African American students are less competent, less capable, and less intelligent. So entrenched is this pattern of thought, that many African Americans actually fear that if they go to school and do poorly that this will 'confirm' the stereotype. As a result, some African Americans score lower than students from other ethnic groups, particularly white students. Their lower performance has been shown to have very little to do with intelligence. It is much more the result of social constructs such as poverty and culture.[22]

Just the awareness that negative stereotypes exist about you can create a strong preoccupation among those who are the target of the stereotype. This preoccupation is generally referred to as "stigma consciousness."[23] For some African Americans, so powerful is the effect of this threat, that they may attribute, at times, a lack of academic success to racism and discrimination. This further perpetuates low academic performance because doing well now seems out of their control. The whole cycle highlights a problem in schools, NOT a problem of intelligence or ability among African Americans (or any other minority).

Students from lower socioeconomic backgrounds and from families in which they have received little support for education from their parents may attribute lack of academic success to their family backgrounds. A lack of academic skills due to circumstances such as poverty, bad neighborhoods (and crime), and negative parenting practices has a significant negative impact on the educational experiences and skills of students, particularly minority students. K-12 and higher education schools have been trying to make system-wide changes to improve education and equal opportunity for all students.[24] However, I always encourage students to focus on what they can influence, themselves, from now on. Dwelling constantly on your past and blaming it for your present will simply get in the way of your future. I fully respect the impact our past has on who we are right now, but there comes a time to make change in your life as it is, rather than tethering (i.e., tying) yourself to your past. I also understand how "the system" can perpetuate and even create barriers. This is wrong and we need to work together to effect positive changes!

Culture and PK2SS #3 – Achievement Goals and Interest

The goals that you set for your education and your future career are a function of your cultural upbringing. It is not hard to imagine that your goals are influenced by the individualistic and collectivist cultures distinction. While we, in Western cultures, set goals for individual achievement, people in other cultures may approach education quite differently. In fact, one's personal goals could reflect a desire to help others meet their goals. Personal goals and group goals are interwoven; much like in the collectivist cultures themselves, personal and group goals are connected.[25]

Another key difference in how people from different cultures set and approach their goals involves their sense of control (sometimes referred to as "agency" in the literature). People from individualistic cultures generally try to use their personal qualities to impact social situations. Alternatively, people from many collectivist cultures tend to focus control on themselves – they control their internal or personal qualities in order to fit in with social situations.[26]

The different achievement goal orientations we considered (i.e., mastery, performance-approach, and performance-avoidance) appear to exist across different cultures. For example, one study demonstrated that both European-American and Asian-American students who were high in the need for achievement tended to have a mastery or a performance-approach achievement goal orientation, while those high in the need to avoid failure tended to have a performance-approach or a performance-avoidance achievement goal orientation.[27,28] A study of over 1,800 seventh grade students in China found the performance goal orientation to be most prevalent, although both performance and mastery goals were explained to be valued in Chinese schools.[29]

Culture and PK2SS #4 – Self-efficacy

Self-efficacy is confidence in your ability to accomplish something. In Western psychology and education, this is a core concept related to success. Once again, however, culture has a significant influence on its meaning. Students from individualistic cultures tend to believe they are very competent and often overestimate their abilities. Conversely, students with Asian heritage seem to focus less on self-efficacy and more on the importance of doing well on any given task.[30] A study of 8th grade students in Japan and the United States found that the Japanese students in the study, compared to American students, showed high math achievement but had lower math confidence.[31] Sometimes lower self-efficacy, regardless of culture, can lead to a fear of failure. Remember from PK2SS #3, achievement goals, that students with a performance-avoidance orientation are motivated to avoid tasks, often because of a fear of failure. This is based largely on research with students in Western cultures. This pattern is not the case in non-Western cultures. For example, fear of failure has been found to be a predictor of high academic achievement in Japan.[32] These are just a few examples of how self-efficacy can affect people differently depending on their cultural backgrounds.

The importance of self-efficacy on student performance is very clear, as you read in PK2SS #4. This importance may be even truer for students of color and other minority groups. For example, Terrell Strayhorn explained that many students arrive at college underprepared and that more minority, first-generation, and low-income students require remedial education than other students. He suggested that summer bridge programs should endeavor to help students prepare for college in two important ways. First, such programs help increase college readiness by increasing academic skills. Second, these programs help students develop more confidence in their abilities which translate into higher levels of academic performance.[33]

Personally, I believe it is important to understand students' backgrounds so that I can know more about their level of confidence. That way, I can help all students maximize their performance. Remember, success experiences are the best way to increase your confidence!

Culture and PK2SS #5 – Metacognition

As you saw previously, this is all about HOW you think. It involves your level of awareness and responsiveness to your thoughts before, during, and after a task. Your metacognitive knowledge, experiences, and skills are significantly influenced by beliefs (PK2SS #1). As I am now pointing out, culture influences your beliefs. This is yet another example of how culture brings us full circle...back to beliefs.

Culture and PK2SS #6 – Self-regulated Learning

Self-regulated learning focuses on students need to set goals, maintain motivation, and control their behavior in pursuit of their goals. This includes evaluating what strategies produce desired results and which do not. What exactly motivates people, as you have seen, varies a lot from one culture to the next. Response to feedback is another aspect of SRL with marked differences depending upon your culture. For example, people from collectivist cultures often view criticism and negative feedback as more accurate, credible, and helpful than praise. This lies in stark contrast to the Western desire to promote the positive and preserve self-esteem. Interestingly, a 1996 study demonstrated that high school students in Australia and students in Japan both frequently failed to use feedback on tests and other work at all.[34] I certainly hope that, at this point, you are convinced to seek out and use feedback from your instructors!

Culture and PK2SS #7 – Thinking Errors

With respect to understanding thinking errors, there are many differences to consider when examining the influence of culture. The self-serving bias and fundamental attribution error appear to be Western constructions. The hindsight bias, however, is more prevalent in some Eastern cultures. (If you are having trouble remembering what those errors are, please go back and quickly review PK2SS #7.) And from my own interpretation, the Dunning Kruger effect is something based on an individual's lack of understanding and concomitant ignorance in evaluating others. That is based on the notion that we evaluate others by referencing our own knowledge. In collectivist cultures, knowledge is about understanding others and anticipating their needs. As such, I would personally expect the Dunning Kruger effect to be less prevalent in non-Western cultures. That might make a good hypothesis for a research study!

Culture and Motivation

While not designated as an independent PK2SS, remember that motivation is an important determinant of what goals we set and pursue, the tenacity with which we pursue them, and how we subsequently explain the results we get. Yes, in that statement I have encompassed motivation, goals, and attributions. I think you might recognize those ideas as some of the PK2SS? ☺

There is a clear Western bias in our discussion with respect to our motivations, goals, and attributions. Generally speaking (and bluntly speaking), this bias is ME ME ME! What do **I** want? How am **I** special/unique? What grade did **I** get? What job do **I** want? How much money do **I** want and what toys can **I** buy with that money? What makes ME happy?

In my opinion (that is ironic), these questions are not the problem. The problem shows up when we fail to consider that there are many points-of-view when answering these questions. You may be motivated to have a career where you can make a lot of money and have everything you dreamed about as a kid. You may think that college and your career are displays of your personal qualities, such as effort, insight, and intelligence. However, someone else may also be motivated to have the same career but be more motivated to provide for her extended family and make a contribution to society.

People from individualistic cultures are motivated by "actions that allow expression of one's important self-defining, inner attributes" but people from collectivist cultures are more likely motivated by "actions that enhance or foster one's relatedness or connection to others."[35] Another interesting difference can be seen in terms of what people find intrinsically motivating. An interesting example of this came from research that found elementary age Asian-American students were more intrinsically motivated when a task was chosen for them by someone else, compared to Anglo American students who showed more intrinsic motivation when allowed to make their own choice.[36]

Of course, you can do both. But the overall perspectives and motivations of people can differ a great deal, as you see, based on culture.

Final Thoughts

What is particularly interesting about our entire consideration of the Psychological Keys to Student Success is that each key is related to all of the other keys. The entire concept demonstrates INTERDEPENDENCE. All of the concepts considered in this book are related. So, even if you are from a culture that thrives on personal fulfillment and individual achievement, within yourself, the true key to personal success is a system of relationships between the psychological qualities and skills we have considered. How ironic is that?

WHAT IT MEANS TO ME

Helping others is my primary motivation. That is why I worked as a psychometrist. That is why I am a teacher. That is why I wrote this book.

I believe that pretty much everything related to school should be thought of as a skill. Reading is a skill. Writing is a skill. Math is a skill. Studying for different types of exams is a skill. If you share these beliefs with me, you have a growth mindset because skills are something that can be developed.

Mistakes are natural. I make them all the time. Mistakes are usually correctable as long as you are willing to learn from your experience. Personally, the thought of blaming my mistakes on others is just wrong. If I own my mistakes, I can correct them. When I do well, there are many factors that contribute to my successes. I am hard-working, conscientious, dedicated, and enjoy learning. There are factors outside of me that are also helpful such as having supportive colleagues, friends, and family. Do you like my attributions?

I love to learn. I am also competitive. There have also been times in my life that I have been afraid to fail. So, I have experienced all of the achievement goal orientations. However, the first two are my main motivators. Learning and being knowledgeable are wonderful in and of themselves. Kicking some academic butt is fun too!

Self-efficacy comes from personal experience, watching others, and support and encouragement from others. In my life I have been very fortunate to have all of the above. I have experienced success based on my efforts. I have had great mentors. Above all, I have been blessed with unconditional love and support from my family.

As a counselor and a teacher, being aware of your own thought processes is essential. I believe that, in order to be successful, I must constantly monitor and evaluate my thinking. I really wish someone would have taught me about the importance of metacognition when I was in school. My studying and efforts would have been more focused and efficient.

Without knowing it, I was always a self-regulated learner. No one had to tell me and remind me of what needed to be done. I read and researched tirelessly to answer my own questions. I also paid very close attention to every bit of written feedback I got so that I would benefit from the vast experience of my professors. When I didn't understand something, I asked questions.

As I did the research for this book, I ended up teaching myself a lot about thinking errors. That led me to a realization: I now see that I was guilty of many thinking errors when I was in school. Again, I wish someone would have taught me about this stuff. In the past two years I have become extremely aware of my own errors (that's metacognitive knowledge, by the way). Now, I work to catch them and correct them (I have an internal locus of control).

I am very lucky to work at a school with an amazingly diverse student body. Each day, I learn from my students about how the experience of school varies markedly based on who they are. Culture shapes all of us. Things like previous schooling, neighborhoods, family background, traditions, religion, and sexual orientation all matter. Borders exist between countries, not people. We are all interdependent: I believe that one of the greatest individual achievements happens when a person understands, respects, and works together with others!

Thank you for reading the Psychological Keys to Student Success. It is my sincere hope that you have learned some thinking skills that will help you in the pursuit of your academic and career goals. I wish you the very best.

NOTES

Introduction to the Psychological Keys to Student Success

1 Quotation from page 7 of Gall, M.D., Gall, J. P., Jacobsen, D. R., and Bullock, T. L. (1990). *Tools for learning: A guide to teaching study skills*. Alexandria, VA: Association for Supervision and Curriculum Development.

2 Research by Chapel (1995) as cited on page 172 of Weissberg, N. C., Owen, D. R., Jenkins, A. H., and Harburg, E. (2003). The incremental variance problem: Enhancing the predictability of academic success in an urban, commuter institution. *Genetic, Social, and General Psychology Monographs, 129*(2), 153-180.

3 Lotkowski, V. A., Robbins, S. B., and Noeth, R. J. (2004). The role of academic and non academic factors in improving college retention. ACT Policy Report. *American College Testing ACT Inc.*

4 Brown, S. D., Tramayne, S., Hoxha, D., Telander, K., Fan, X., and Lent, R. W. (2008). Social cognitive predictors of college students' academic performance and persistence: A meta-analytic path analysis. *Journal of Vocational Behavior, 72*(3), 298-308.

5 Pascarella, E. T., Wolniak, G. C., and Pierson, C. T. (2003). Influences on community college students' educational plans. *Research in Higher Education, 44*(3), 301-314.

6 The predictors of academic success are many and are complex. General cognitive ability (intelligence) is, undeniably, one of those factors. There is a tome of research in that area and it was not my intention to review it in this book. However, for some interesting examples, one might consider Kuncel, N. R., Hezlett, S. A., and Ones, D. S. (2004). Academic performance, career potential, creativity, and job performance: Can one construct predict them all? *Journal of Personality and Social Psychology, 86*(1), 148. Another interesting study is Furnham, A. (2012). Learning styles, personality traits and intelligence as predictors of college academic performance. *Individual Differences Research, 10*(3), 117-128. See also Higgins, D. M., Peterson, J. B., Pihl, R. O., and Lee, A. G. (2007). Prefrontal cognitive ability, intelligence, Big Five personality, and the prediction of advanced academic and workplace

performance. *Journal of Personality and Social Psychology, 93*(2), 298-319. For consideration of "academic ability" and its relationship to achievement, see Harackiewicz, J. M., Barron, K. E., Tauer, J. M., and Elliot, A. J. (2002). Predicting success in college: A longitudinal study of achievement goals and ability measures as predictors of interest and performance from freshman year through graduation. *Journal of Educational Psychology, 94*(3), 562-575.

7 Corno, L., and Mandinach, E. B. (2004). What we have learned about student engagement in the past twenty years. In Dennis M. McInerney and Shawn Van Etten (Eds.), *Big Theories Revisited* (Vol. 4; pp. 297-326). USA: Information Age Publishing.

8 McKenzie, K., Gow, K., and Schweitzer, R. (2004). Exploring first-year academic achievement through structural equation modelling. *Higher Education Research & Development, 23*(1), 95-112.

Motivation – Why It Is Not One of the PK2SS

1 Quotation from pages 80-81 of Murray, H. A. (1938). *Explorations in Personality*. New York: Oxford University Press.

2 For more explanation of these ideas, see McClelland, D. C., Atkinson, J. W., Clark, R. A., and Lowell, E. L. (1953). *The Achievement Motive*. New York: Appleton–Century–Crofts.

3 For more explanation of these ideas, see Atkinson, J. W. (1957). Motivational determinants of risk-taking behavior. *Psychological Review, 64*, 359-372.

4 Elliot, A. J., and Sheldon, K. M. (1997). Avoidance achievement motivation: A personal goals analysis. *Journal of Personality and Social Psychology, 73*(1), 171-185.

5 For example, see Martin, A. J., Marsh, H. W., and Debus, R. L. (2001). Self-handicapping and defensive pessimism: Exploring a model of predictors and outcomes from a self-protection perspective. *Journal of Educational Psychology, 93*(1), 87-102.

6 For example, see Thompson, T., Davidson, J. A., and Barber, J. G. (1995). Self-worth protection in achievement motivation: Performance effects and attributional behavior. *Journal of Educational Psychology, 87*(4), 598-610.

7 Covington, M. V. (2000). Goal theory, motivation, and school achievement: An integrative review. *Annual Review of*

Psychology, 51(1), 171-200.

8 Ajzen, I. (1991). The theory of planned behavior. *Organizational Behavior and Human Decision Processes, 50,* 179-211.

9 Deci, E. L., and Ryan, R. M. (1987). The support of autonomy and the control of behavior. *Journal of Personality and Social Psychology, 53*(6), 1024-1037.

10 Deci, E. L., and Ryan, R. M. (1987).

11 Quotation from page 1032 of Deci, E. L., and Ryan, R. M. (1987).

12 Quotation from page 628 of Deci, E. L, Koestner, R., and Ryan, R. M. (1999). A meta-analytic review of experiments examining the effects of extrinsic rewards on intrinsic motivation. *Psychological Bulletin, 125*(6), 627-668.

PK2SS #1: Beliefs and Mindset

1 Quotation from page 11 of Perna, L. W., and Thomas, S. L. (2006, July). A framework for reducing the college success gap and promoting success for all. In *National Symposium on Postsecondary Student Success: Spearheading a Dialog on Student Success (pp 1-42).*

2 Parpala, A., Lindblom-Ylänne, S., Komulainen, E., Litmanen, T., and Hirsto, L. (2010). Students' approaches to learning and their experiences of the teaching–learning environment in different disciplines. *British Journal of Educational Psychology, 80*(2), 269-282.

3 Schommer, M. (1993). Comparisons of beliefs about the nature of knowledge and learning among postsecondary students. *Research in Higher Education, 34*(3), 355-370.

4 Dahl, T. I., Bals, M., and Turi, A. L. (2005). Are students' beliefs about knowledge and learning associated with their reported use of learning strategies*? British Journal of Psychology, 75*(2), 257-273.

5 Schommer, M. (1990). Effects of beliefs about the nature of knowledge on comprehension. *Journal of Educational Psychology, 82*(3), 498-504.

6 Schommer, M. (1993).

7 Schommer, M., and Walker, K. (1997). Epistemological beliefs and valuing school: Considerations for college admissions and retention. *Research in Higher Education, 38*(2), 173-186.

8 Quotation from page 269 of Dahl, T. I., et al., (2005).

9 Phan, H. P. (2009). Amalgamation of future time orientation, epistemological beliefs, achievement goals and study strategies: Empirical evidence established. *British Journal of Educational Psychology, 79*(1), 155-173.

10 Grimes, P. W. (2002). The overconfident principles of economics student: An examination of a metacognitive skill. *The Journal of Economic Education, 33*(1), 15-30.

11 For example, see Pekrun, R., Goetz, T., Titz, W., and Perry, R. P. (2002). Academic emotions in students' self-regulated learning and achievement: A program of quantitative and qualitative research. *Educational Psychologist, 37*, 91–106.

12 Ross, M. E., Green, S. B., Salisbury-Glennon, J. D., and Tollefson, N. (2006). College students' study strategies as a function of testing: An investigation into metacognitive self-regulation. *Innovative Higher Education, 30*(5), 361-375.

13 Entwistle, N., and Entwistle, D. (2003). Preparing for examinations: The interplay of memorising and understanding, and the development of knowledge objects. *Higher Education Research and Development*, *22*(1), 19-41.

14 Karpicke, J. D., Butler, A. C., and Roediger III, H. L. (2009). Metacognitive strategies in student learning: Do students practise retrieval when they study on their own? *Memory*, *17*(4), 471-479.

15 Quotation from page 432 of Collier, P. J., and Morgan, D. L. (2008). Is that paper really due today?: Differences in first-generation and traditional college students' understanding of faculty expectations. *Higher Education, 55*(4), 425-446.

16 Valentine, J. C., DuBois, D. L., and Cooper, H. (2004). The relation between self-beliefs and academic achievement: A meta-analytic review. *Educational Psychologist, 39*(2), 111-133.

17 Quotation from page 189 of Ajzen, I. (1991). The theory of planned behavior. *Organizational Behavior and Human Decision Processes, 50*(2), 179-211.

18 Molden, D. C., and Dweck, C. S. (2006). Finding" meaning" in psychology: a lay theories approach to self-regulation, social perception, and social development. *American Psychologist*, *61*(3), 192.

19 Molden, D. C., and Dweck, C. S. (2006).

20 Quotation from page 105 of Boekaerts, M. (1996). Self-regulated learning at the junction of cognition and motivation. *European Psychologist, 1*(2), 100-112.

PK2SS #2: Attributions

1 Quotation from page 3 of Weiner, B. (1979). A theory of motivation for some classroom experiences. *Journal of Educational Psychology, 71*(1), 3-25.

2 Quotation from page 4 of Weiner, B. (1979).

3 Weiner, B. (1979).

4 Shell, D. F., and Husman, J. (2008). Control, motivation, affect, and strategic self-regulation in the college classroom: A multidimensional phenomenon. *Journal of Educational Psychology, 100*(2), 443-459.

5 Perry, R. P., Hladkyj, S., Pekrun, R. H., and Pelletier, S. T. (2001). Academic control and action control in the achievement of college students: A longitudinal field study. *Journal of Educational Psychology, 93*(4), 776-789.

6 Perry, R. P. (2003). Perceived (academic) control and causal thinking in achievement settings. *Canadian Psychology, 44*(4), 312-331.

7 Rotter, J. B. (1966). Generalized expectancies for internal versus external control of reinforcement. *Psychological monographs: General and applied, 80*(1), 1-28.

8 Quotation from page 317 of Linnenbrink, E. A., and Pintrich, P. R. (2002). Motivation as an enabler for academic success. *School Psychology Review, 31*(3), 313-327.

9 According to Weiner, B. (1985). An attributional theory of achievement motivation and emotion. *Psychological Review, 92*(4), 548-573, this is common.

10 Heider, F. (1958). *The psychology of interpersonal relations.* New York: Wiley.

11 Rotter, J. B. (1966). Generalized expectancies for internal versus external control of reinforcement. *Psychological monographs: General and applied, 80*(1), 1-28.

12 Atkinson, J. W. (1964). *An introduction to motivation*. Princeton, N.J.: Van Nostrand.

13 Weiner (1985).

14 Weiner (2010).

15 Schunk, D. H., Meece, J. L., and Pintrich, P. R. (2014). *Motivation in education: Theory, research, and applications* (4th ed.). Upper Saddle River, NJ: Pearson.

PK2SS #3: Achievement Goals and Interest

1 Quotation from page 215 of Urdan, T. C., and Maehr, M. L. (1995). Beyond a two-goal theory of motivation and achievement: A case for social goals. *Review of Educational Research, 65*(3), 213-243.

2 Wentzel, K. R. (2000). What is it that I'm trying to achieve? Classroom goals from a content perspective. *Contemporary Educational Psychology, 25*, 105-115.

3 Miller, R. B., and Brickman, S. J. (2004). A model of future-oriented motivation and self-regulation. *Educational Psychology Review, 16*(1), 9-33.

4 Hulleman, C. S., Schrager, S. M., Bodmann, S. M., and Harackiewicz, J. M. (2010). A meta-analytic review of achievement goal measures: Different labels for the same constructs or different constructs with similar labels? *Psychological Bulletin, 136*(3), 422-449.

5 Quotation from page 261 of Ames, C. (1992). Classrooms: Goals, structures, and student motivation. *Journal of Educational Psychology, 84*(3), 261-271.

6 Quotation from page 423 of Hulleman, et. al. (2010).

7 Quotation from page 94 of Pintrich, P. (2000). An achievement goal theory perspective on issues in motivation terminology, theory, and research. *Contemporary Educational Psychology, 25*(1), 92–104.

8 Ideas in this paragraph are based on Dweck, C. S., and Leggett, E. L. (1988). A social-cognitive approach to motivation and personality. *Psychological Review, 95*, 256–273.

9 Senko, C., Hulleman, C. S., and Harackiewicz, J. M. (2011). Achievement goal theory at the crossroads: Old controversies, current challenges, and new directions. *Educational Psychologist, 46*(1), 26-47.

10 Covington, M. V. (2000). Goal theory, motivation, and school achievement: An integrative review. *Annual Review of Psychology, 51*(1), 171-200.

11 Quotation from page 194 of Schunk, D. H., Meece, J. L., and Pintrich, P. R. (2014). *Motivation in Education* (4th ed.). Upper Saddle River, NJ: Pearson.

12 Grant, H. and Dweck, C. S. (2003). Clarifying achievement goals and their impact. *Journal of Personality and Social Psychology, 85*, 541-553.

13 Weiner, B. (1979). A theory of motivation for some classroom experiences. *Journal of Educational Psychology, 71*(1), 3-25.

14 Ames, C. (1992).

15 Hulleman, et. al. (2010).

16 Senko, C., et. al. (2011).

17 Pekrun R., Elliot, A. J., and Maier, M. A. (2009). Achievement goals and achievement emotions: Testing a model of their joint relations with academic performance. *Journal of Educational Psychology, 101*(1), 115-135.

18 Hulleman, et. al. (2010).

19 Baumeister, R. F., Bratslavsky, E., Finkenauer, C., and Vohs, K. D. (2001). Bad is stronger than good. *Review of General Psychology*, *5*(4), 323-370.

20 Elliot, A. J., and Harackiewicz, J. M. (1996). Approach and avoidance achievement goals and intrinsic motivation: A mediational analysis. *Journal of Personality and Social Psychology, 70*, 461-475.

21 Quotation from page 186 of Covington, M. V. (2000).

22 Research conducted by Senko and Harackiewicz as cited in Brophy, J. (2005). Goal theorists should move on from performance goals. *Educational Psychologist, 40*(3), 167-176.

23 Elliot, A. J., and Church, M. A. (1997). A hierarchical model of approach and avoidance achievement motivation. *Journal of Personality and Social Psychology,72*(1), 218-232.

24 Covington, M. V. (2000).

25 Pekrun R., et. al. (2009).

26 Harackiewicz, J. M., Barron, K. E., Tauer, J. M., and Elliot, A. J. (2002). Predicting success in college: A longitudinal study of achievement goals and ability measures as predictors of interest and performance from freshman year through graduation. *Journal of Educational Psychology*, *94*(3), 562-575.

27 Pintrich, P. R. (2003). A motivational science perspective on the role of student motivation in learning and teaching contexts. *Journal of Educational Psychology*, *95*(4), 667-686.

28 Research by Rathunde as cited in Hidi, S., and Harackiewicz, J. M. (2000). Motivating the academically unmotivated: A critical issue for the 21st century. *Review of Educational Research, 70*(2), 151-179.

29 For a review, see Hidi, S., and Harackiewicz, J. M. (2000).

30 For a review, see Renninger, K. A., and Hidi, S. (2011). Revisiting

the conceptualization, measurement, and generation of interest. *Educational Psychologist, 46*(3), 168-184.

31 Quotation from page 425 of Mitchell, M. (1993). Situational interest: Its multifaceted structure in the secondary school mathematics classroom. *Journal of Educational Psychology, 85*(3), 424-436.

32 For example, see Hulleman, C. S., Godes, O., Hendricks, B. L., and Harackiewicz, J. M. (2010). Enhancing interest and performance with a utility value intervention. *Journal of Educational Psychology, 102*(4), 880-895.

33 Mitchell, M. (1993).

34 Azevedo, R. (2005). Using hypermedia as a metacognitive tool for enhancing student learning? The role of self-regulated learning. *Educational Psychologist, 40*(4), 199-209.

35 Son, L. K., and Metcalfe, J. (2000). Metacognitive and control strategies in study-time allocation. *Journal of Experimental Psychology: Learning, Memory, and Cognition, 26*(1), 204-221.

PK2SS #4: Self-efficacy

1 Eccles, J. S., and Wigfield, A. (2002). Motivational beliefs, values, and goals. *Annual Review of Psychology, 53*, 109-132.

2 Dennison, J. J. A., Zarrett, N. R., and Eccles, J. S. (2007). I like to do it, I'm able, and I know I am: Longitudinal couplings between domain-specific achievement, self-concept, and interest. *Child Development, 78*(2), 430-447.

3 Zimmerman, B. J. (1995). Self-regulation involves more than metacognition: A social cognitive perspective. *Educational Psychologist, 30*(4), 217-221.

4 Pintrich, P. R. (2003). A motivational science perspective on the role of student motivation in learning and teaching contexts. *Journal of Educational Psychology, 95*(4), 667-686.

5 Pajares, F. (2002). Gender and perceived self-efficacy in self-regulated learning. *Theory Into Practice, 41*(2), 116-125.

6 Pintrich, P.R. (2003).

7 Zimmerman, B. J. and Cleary, T. J. (2006). Adolescents' development of personal agency: The role of self-efficacy beliefs and self-regulatory skill. In F. Pajares and T. Urdan (Eds.), *Self-efficacy beliefs of adolescents* (pp. 45-70). Greenwich, CT: Information Age Publishing.

8 "Selection processes," paragraph 1 of Bandura, A. (1994). Self-efficacy. In V. S. Ramachaudran (Ed.). *Encyclopedia of human behavior* (Vol. 4, pp. 71-81). New York: Academic Press. Retrieved from http://www.uky.edu/~eushe2/Bandura/BanEncy.html

9 Quotation from page 542 of Cleary, T. J., and Zimmerman, B. J. (2004). Self-regulation empowerment program: A school-based program to enhance self-regulated and self-motivated cycles of student learning. *Psychology in the Schools, 41*(5), 537-550.

10 Robbins, S. B., Lauver, K., Le, H., Davis, D., Langley, R., and Carlstrom, A. (2004). Do psychosocial and study skill factors predict college outcomes? A meta-analysis. *Psychological Bulletin, 130*(2), 261.

11 Bandura, A. (1977). Self-efficacy: Toward a unifying theory of behavioral change. *Psychological Review, 84*(2), 191-215.

12 Quotation on page 195 of Bandura, A. (1977).

13 Quotation on page 27 of Miller, R. B., and Brickman, S. J. (2004). A model of future-oriented motivation and self-regulation. *Educational Psychology Review, 16*(1), 9-33.

14 Quotation on page 9 of Weiner, B. (1979). A theory of motivation for some classroom experiences. *Journal of Educational Psychology, 71*(1), 3-25.

15 Bandura, A. (1977).

16 For an example of an empirical study demonstrating the effect of watching non-experts perform a behavior on another's self-efficacy, see Schunk, D. H., and Hanson, A. R. (1985). Peer models: Influence on children's self-efficacy and achievement. *Journal of Educational Psychology, 77*, 313-322.

17 Bandura, A. (1994). Self-efficacy. In V. S. Ramachaudran (Ed.). *Encyclopedia of human behavior* (Vol. 4, pp. 71-81). New York: Academic Press. Retrieved from http://www.uky.edu/~eushe2/Bandura/BanEncy.html

18 Senko, C., Hulleman, C. S., and Harackiewicz, J. M. (2011). Achievement goal theory at the crossroads: Old controversies, current challenges, and new directions. *Educational Psychologist, 46*(1), 26-47.

19 Quotation on page 315 of Linnenbrink, E. A., and Pintrich, P. R. (2002). Motivation as an enabler for academic success. *School Psychology Review, 31*(3), 313-327.

20 Schunk, D. H. (1991). Self-efficacy and academic motivation. *Educational Psychologist, 26*(3&4), 207-231.

21 Zimmerman, B. J. and Cleary, T. J. (2006).

22 Zimmerman, B. J. and Cleary, T. J. (2006).

23 Schraw, G., Crippen, K. J., and Hartley, K. (2006). Promoting self-regulation in science education: Metacognition as part of a broader perspective on learning. *Research in Science Education, 36*, 111-139.

24 Pintrich, P.R. (2003).

25 Corno, L., and Mandinach, E. B. (2004). What we have learned about student engagement in the past twenty years. In Dennis M. McInerney and Shawn Van Etten (Eds.), *Big Theories Revisited* (Vol. 4; pp. 297-326). USA: Information Age Publishing.

26 Brophy, J. (2005). Goal theorists should move on from performance goals. *Educational Psychologist, 40*(3), 167-176.

27 Locke, E. A., and Latham, G. P. (2002). Building a practically useful theory of goal setting and task motivation: A 35-year odyssey. *American Psychologist, 57*(9), 705–717.

PK2SS #5: Metacognition

1 Quotation from page 136 of Lew, M. D. N., Alwis, W. A. M., and Schmidt, H. G. (2010). Accuracy of students' self-assessment and their beliefs about its utility. *Assessment & Evaluation in Higher Education, 35*(2), 135-156.

2 Flavell, J. H. (1979). Metacognition and cognitive monitoring: A new area of cognitive-developmental inquiry. *American Psychologist, 34*(10), 906-911.

3 Hamachek, 1995, as noted on page 342 of Schleiger, L. L. F., and Dull, R. B. (2009). Metacognition and performance in the accounting classroom. *Issues in Accounting Education, 24*(3), 339-367.

4 Quotation from page 5 of Paris, S. G. and Winograd, P. (2003). *The role of self-regulated learning in contextual teaching: Principles and practices for teacher preparation*. A commissioned paper for the U.S. Department of Education project Preparing Teachers to Use Contextual Teaching and Learning Strategies To Improve Student Success In and Beyond School. Retrieved from: http://files.eric.ed.gov/fulltext/ED479905.pdf

5 Quotation from page 16 of Grimes, P. W. (2002). The overconfident principles of economics student: An

examination of a metacognitive skill. *Journal of Economic Education, 33*(1), 15-30.

6 Efklides, A. (2011). Interactions of metacognition with motivation and affect in self-regulated learning: The MASRL model. *Educational Psychologist, 46*(1), 6-25.

7 Paris, S. G. and Winograd, P. (2003). The role of self-regulated learning in contextual teaching: Principles and practices for teacher preparation. A commissioned paper for the U.S. Department of Education project Preparing Teachers to Use Contextual Teaching and Learning Strategies To Improve Student Success In and Beyond School. Retrieved from: http://files.eric.ed.gov/fulltext/ED479905.pdf

8 Efklides, A. (2008). Metacognition: Defining its facets and levels of functioning in relation to self-regulation and co-regulation. *European Psychologist, 13*(4), 277-287.

9 Quotation from page 205 of Azevedo, R. (2005). Using hypermedia as a metacognitive tool for enhancing student learning? The role of self-regulated learning. *Educational Psychologist, 40*(4), 199-209.

10 Tanner, K. D. (2012). Promoting student metacognition. *CBE-Life Sciences Education, 11*(2), 113-120.

11 Pintrich, P. R. (2002). The role of metacognitive knowledge in learning, teaching, and assessing. *Theory Into Practice, 41*(4), 219-225.

12 Kruger, J., and Dunning, D. (1999). Unskilled and unaware of it: how difficulties in recognizing one's own incompetence lead to inflated self-assessments. *Journal of Personality and Social Psychology, 77*(6), 1121-1134.

13 Information and chart from page 120 of Schraw, G. (1998). Promoting general metacognitive awareness. *Instructional Science, 26*(1-2), 113-125.

14 The ideas in this paragraph are related to insights offered in Efklides, A. (2011).

15 Pintrich, P. R., and De Groot, E. V. (1990). Motivational and self-regulated learning components of classroom academic performance. *Journal of Educational Psychology, 82*(1), 33-40.

16 Quotation from page 431 of McMahon, M., and Luca, J. (2001, December). Assessing students' self-regulatory skills. In *annual conference of the Australasian Society for Computers in Learning in Tertiary Education, Melbourne, Australia. (ERIC Document*

Reproduction Service No. ED467960).

PK2SS #6: Self-regulated Learning

1 Baumeister, R. F., Bratslavsky, E., Muraven, M., and Tice, D. M. (1998). Ego depletion: is the active self a limited resource? *Journal of Personality and Social Psychology, 74*(5), 1252-1265.

2 Kennett, D. J., and Keefer, K. (2006). Impact of learned resourcefulness and theories of intelligence on academic achievement of university students: An integrated approach. *Educational Psychology, 26*(3), 441-457.

3 When structure is provided as part of a scaffolded approach to learning, as suggested by Lev Vygotsky, it can facilitate learning. However, in this approach, structure and support is gradually removed as the student gains confidence and ability. My comment here is geared toward teachers who constantly give reminders, extend deadlines, threaten consequences, cajole, and otherwise provide extensive extrinsic motivators for students.

4 Zimmerman, B. J. and Cleary, T. J. (2006). Adolescents' development of personal agency: The role of self-efficacy beliefs and self-regulatory skill. In F. Pajares and T. Urdan (Eds.), *Self-efficacy beliefs of adolescents* (pp. 45-70). Greenwich, CT: Information Age Publishing.

5 Schraw, G., Crippen, K. J., and Hartley, K. (2006). Promoting self-regulation in science education: Metacognition as part of a broader perspective on learning. *Research in Science Education, 36*, 111-139.

6 Quotation from page 20 of Klassen, R. M. (2010). Confidence to manage learning: The self-efficacy for self-regulated learning of early adolescents with learning disabilities. *Learning Disability Quarterly, 33*, 19-30.

7 For a review, see Puustinen, M., and Pulkkinen, L. (2001). Models of self-regulated learning: A review. *Scandinavian Journal of Educational Research, 45*(3), 269-286.

8 Pintrich, P. R., and De Groot, E. V. (1990). Motivational and self-regulated learning components of classroom academic performance. *Journal of Educational Psychology, 82*(1), 33-40.

9 Quotation from page 404 of Dinsmore, D. L., Alexander, P. A., and Loughlin, S. M. (2008). Focusing the conceptual lens on metacognition, self-regulation, and self-regulated learning.

Educational Psychology Review, 20(4), 391-409.

10 Pintrich, P. R. (2004). A conceptual framework for assessing motivation and self-regulated learning in college students. *Educational Psychology Review, 16*(4), 385-407.

11 Boekaerts, M., and Cascallar, E. (2006). How far have we moved toward the integration of theory and practice in self-regulation? *Educational Psychology Review, 18*(3), 199-210.

12 Quotation from page 180 of Covington, M. V. (2000). Goal theory, motivation, and school achievement: An integrative review. *Annual Review of Psychology, 51*(1), 171-200.

13 Risemberg, R., and Zimmerman, B. J. (1992). Self-regulated learning in gifted students. *Roeper Review, 15*(2), 98-101.

14 Quotation from page 4 of Zimmerman, B. J. (1990). Self-regulated learning and academic achievement: An overview. *Educational Psychologist, 25*(1), 3-17.

15 Paris, S. G. and Winograd, P. (2003). The role of self-regulated learning in contextual teaching: Principles and practices for teacher preparation. A commissioned paper for the U.S. Department of Education project Preparing Teachers to Use Contextual Teaching and Learning Strategies To Improve Student Success In and Beyond School. Retrieved from: http://files.eric.ed.gov/fulltext/ED479905.pdf

16 Cleary, T. J., and Zimmerman, B. J. (2004). Self-regulation empowerment program: A school-based program to enhance self-regulated and self-motivated cycles of student learning. *Psychology in the Schools, 41*(5), 537-550.

17 Pajares, F. (2002). Gender and perceived self-efficacy in self-regulated learning. *Theory Into Practice, 41*(2), 116-125.

18 Covington, M. V. (2000).

19 Pintrich, P. R. (2004).

20 Schunk, D. H. (2005). Self-regulated learning: The educational legacy of Paul R. Pintrich. *Educational Psychologist, 40*(2), 85-94.

21 Azevedo, R. (2005). Using hypermedia as a metacognitive tool for enhancing student learning? The role of self-regulated learning. *Educational Psychologist, 40*(4), 199-209.

22 Quotation from page 60 of Zimmerman, B. J. and Cleary, T. J. (2006).

23 Azevedo, R. (2005).

24 Quotation from page 73 of Zimmerman, B. J. (1998). Academic studying and the development of personal skill: A self-regulatory

perspective. *Educational Psychologist, 33*(2/3), 73-86.

25 These are outlined in Zimmerman, B. J. (1994). Dimensions of academic self-regulation: A conceptual framework for education. In D. H. Schunk and B. J. Zimmerman (Eds.), *Self-regulation of learning and performance: Issues and educational applications* (pp. 3-21). Hilldale, NJ: Lawrence Erlbaum Associates.

26 Quotation from page 190 of Wolters, C. A. (2003). Regulation of motivation: Evaluating an underemphasized aspect of self-regulated learning. *Educational Psychologist, 38*(4), 189-205.

27 Boekaerts, M., and Corno, L. (2005). Self-regulation in the classroom: A perspective on assessment and intervention. *Applied Psychology: An International Review, 54*(2), 199-231.

28 Miller, R. B., and Brickman, S. J. (2004). A model of future-oriented motivation and self-regulation. *Educational Psychology Review, 16*(1), 9-33.

29 Miller, R. B., and Brickman, S. J. (2004).

30 Sitzmann, T., and Ely, K. (2011). A meta-analysis of self-regulated learning in work-related training and educational attainment: what we know and where we need to go. *Psychological Bulletin, 137*(3), 421-442.

31 Locke, E. A., and Latham, G. P. (2002). Building a practically useful theory of goal setting and task motivation. *American Psychologist, 57*(9), 705-717.

32 Boekaerts, M., and Corno, L. (2005).

33 Research by Ruvolo and Markus (1992) as cited in Valentine, J. C., DuBois, D. L., and Cooper, H. (2004). The relation between self-beliefs and academic achievement: A meta-analytic review. *Educational Psychologist, 39*(2), 111-133.

34 Quotation from page 109 of Boekaerts, M. (1996). Self-regulated learning at the junction of cognition and motivation. *European Psychologist, 1*(2), 100-112.

35 Puustinen, M., and Pulkkinen, L. (2001).

36 Sitzmann, T., and Ely, K. (2011).

37 Eccles, J. (1983). Expectancies, values and academic behaviors. In J. T. Spence (Ed.), *Achievement and Achievement Motives* (pp. 75-146). San Francisco: Freeman.

38 Pintrich, P. R., and De Groot, E. V. (1990).

39 Wolters, C. A. (2003).

40 Renninger, K. A., and Hidi, S. (2011). Revisiting the conceptualization, measurement, and generation of

interest. *Educational Psychologist, 46*(3), 168-184.
41 Boekaerts, M., and Corno, L. (2005).
42 Boekaerts, M. (1996).
43 Quotation from page 7 of Zimmerman, B. J. (1990).
44 Pintrich, P. R. (2003). A motivational science perspective on the role of student motivation in learning and teaching contexts. *Journal of Educational Psychology, 95*(4), 667-686.
45 Quotation from page 428 of Collier, P. J., and Morgan, D. L. (2008). Is that paper really due today? Differences in first-generation and traditional college students' understanding of faculty expectations. *Higher Education, 55*(4), 425-446.
46 Acher, J., and Scevak, J. J. (1998). Enhancing students' motivation to learn: Achievement goals in university classrooms. *Educational Psychology, 18*(2), 205-223.
47 Quotation from page 53 of Zimmerman, B. J. and Cleary, T. J. (2006).
48 Topping, K. (1998). Peer assessment between students in colleges and universities. *Review of Educational Research, 68*(3), 249-276.
49 Zimmerman, B. J., and Martinez-Pons, M. (1988). Construct validation of a strategy model of student self-regulated learning. *Journal of Educational Psychology, 80*(3), 284-290.
50 Zimmerman, B. J. (1998).
51 Quotation from page 202 of Azevedo, R. (2005).

PK2SS #7: Thinking Errors

1 Crosby, R. A., and Yarber, W. L. (2001). Perceived versus actual knowledge about correct condom use among US adolescents: results from a national study. *Journal of Adolescent Health, 28*(5), 415-420.
2 Risucci, D. A., Tortolani, A. J., and Ward, R. J. (1989). Ratings of surgical residents by self, supervisors and peers. *Surgery, Gynecology & Obstetrics, 169*(6), 519-526.
3 Bol, L., and Hacker, D. J. (2001). A comparison of the effects of practice tests and traditional review on performance and calibration. *The Journal of Experimental Education, 69*(2), 133-151.
4 Fischhoff, B., Slovic, P., and Lichtenstein, S. (1977). Knowing with certainty: The appropriateness of extreme confidence. *Journal of Experimental Psychology: Human Perception and Performance, 3*(4), 552-564.

5 Quotation from page 70 of Bjork, R. A. (1999). Assessing our own competence: Heuristics and illusions. In D. Gopher and A. Koriat (Eds.), *Attention and performance XVII: Cognitive regulation of performance: Interaction of theory and application* (pp. 435-459). Cambridge, MA: MIT Press.

6 Quotation from page 1121 of Kruger, J., and Dunning, D. (1999). Unskilled and unaware of it: how difficulties in recognizing one's own incompetence lead to inflated self-assessments. *Journal of Personality and Social Psychology, 77*(6), 1121-1134.

7 Sheldon, O. J., Dunning, D., and Ames, D. R. (2014). Emotionally unskilled, unaware, and uninterested in learning more: Reactions to feedback about deficits in emotional intelligence. *Journal of Applied Psychology, 99*(1), 1-13.

8 Karpicke, J. D., Butler, A. C., and Roediger III, H. L. (2009). Metacognitive strategies in student learning: Do students practise retrieval when they study on their own? *Memory, 17*(4), 471-479.

9 Dunning, D., Johnson, K., Ehrlinger, J., and Kruger, J. (2003). Why people fail to recognize their own incompetence. *Current Directions in Psychological Science, 12*(3), 83-87.

10 Hacker, D. J., Bol, L., Horgan, D. D., and Rakow, E. A. (2000). Test prediction and performance in a classroom context. *Journal of Educational Psychology,92*(1), 160-170.

11 Sinkavich, F. J. (1995). Performance and metamemory: Do students know what they don't know? *Journal of Instructional Psychology, 22*, 77-87.

12 Carter, T. J., and Dunning, D. (2008). Faulty Self-Assessment: Why evaluating one's own competence is an intrinsically difficult task. *Social and Personality Psychology Compass, 2*(1), 346-360.

13 Shaw III, J. S. (1996). Increases in eyewitness confidence resulting from postevent questioning. *Journal of Experimental Psychology Applied, 2*(2), 126-146.

14 Chemers, M. M., Hu, L. T., and Garcia, B. F. (2001). Academic self-efficacy and first year college student performance and adjustment. *Journal of Educational Psychology, 93*(1), 55-64.

15 The survey was reported in Dunning, D., Heath, C., and Suls, J. M. (2004). Flawed self-assessment: Implications for health, education, and the workplace. *Psychological Science in the Public Interest, 5*(3), 69-106.

16 Pintrich, P. R. (2003). A motivational science perspective on the role of student motivation in learning and teaching contexts.

Journal of Educational Psychology, 95(4), 667-686.
17 Caputo, D., and Dunning, D. (2005). What you don't know: The role played by errors of omission in imperfect self-assessments. *Journal of Experimental Social Psychology, 41*(5), 488-505.
18 Dunning, D., Heath, C., and Suls, J. M. (2004).
19 Carter, T. J., and Dunning, D. (2008).
20 Carter, T. J., and Dunning, D. (2008).
21 Dunning, D., Heath, C., and Suls, J. M. (2004).
22 Bjork, R. A. (1999).
23 Dunning, D., Heath, C., and Suls, J. M. (2004).
24 Dunning, D., Heath, C., and Suls, J. M. (2004).
25 Dunlosky, J., and Hertzog, C. (1998). Training programs to improve learning in later adulthood: Helping older adults educate themselves. In D. J. Hacker, J. Dunlosky, and A. C. Graesser (Eds.), *Metacognition in Educational Theory and Practice (pp.* 249-275). Mahwah, NJ: Erlbaum.
26 Thiede, K. W., and Dunlosky, J. (1999). Toward a general model of self-regulated study: An analysis of selection of items for study and self-paced study time. *Journal of Experimental Psychology: Learning, Memory, and Cognition*, *25*(4), 1024-1037.
27 Son, L. K., and Metcalfe, J. (2000). Metacognitive and control strategies in study-time allocation. *Journal of Experimental Psychology: Learning, Memory, and Cognition*, *26*(1), 204-221.
28 Buehler, R., Griffin, D., and Ross, M. (2002). Inside the planning fallacy: The causes and consequences of optimistic time predictions. In T. Gilovich, D. Griffin, and D. Kahneman (Eds.), *Heuristics and biases: The psychology of intuitive judgment* (pp. 251-270). Cambridge, England: Cambridge University Press.
29 Quotation from page 77 of Dunning, D., Heath, C., and Suls, J. M. (2004).
30 Pintrich, P. R. (2003).
31 Quotation from page 352 of Carter, T. J., and Dunning, D. (2008).
32 Pintrich, P. R. (2003).
33 Hassel, H., and Lourey, J. (2005). The dea(r)th of student responsibility. *College Teaching*, *53*(1), 2-13.

PK2SS #8: The Influence of Culture

1 Masuda, T. and Nisbett, R. E. (2001). Attending holistically versus analytically: Comparing the context sensitivity of Japanese and

Americans. *Journal of Personality and Social Psychology, 81*(5), 922-934.

2 Quotation from page 863 of De Castella, K., Byrne, D., and Covington, M. (2013). Unmotivated or motivated to fail? A cross-cultural study of achievement motivation, fear of failure, and student disengagement. *Journal of Educational Psychology, 105*(3), 861-880.

3 Stephens, N. M., Fryberg, S. A., Markus, H. R., Johnson, C. S., and Covarrubias, R. (2012). Unseen disadvantage: how American universities' focus on independence undermines the academic performance of first-generation college students. *Journal of Personality and Social Psychology, 102*(6), 1178.

4 Quotation from page 463 of Myers, D. G. (2014). *Exploring Psychology* (9th ed.). New York, NY: Worth.

5 Quotation from page 12 of Matsumoto, D., and Juang, L. (2008). *Culture and Psychology* (4th ed.). Belmont, CA: Thomson Wadsworth.

6 Nisbett, R. E., Peng, K., Choi, I., and Norenzayan, A. (2001). Culture and systems of thought: holistic versus analytic cognition. *Psychological Review, 108*(2), 291.

7 Fyans, L. J., Salili, F., Maehr, M. L., and Desai, K. A. (1983). A cross-cultural exploration into the meaning of achievement. *Journal of Personality and Social Psychology, 44*(5), 1000-1013.

8 Quotation from page 459 of Plaut, V. C., and Markus, H. R. (2005). The "inside" story. A cultural-historical analysis of being smart and motivated, American style. In Andrew Elliot and Carol Dweck (Eds). *Handbook of Competence and Motivation*. (pp.457-488). New York: Guilford.

9 Plaut, V. C., and Markus, H. R. (2005).

10 Fordham, S., and Ogbu, J. U. (1986). Black students' school success: Coping with the "burden of 'acting white'". *The Urban Review, 18*(3), 176-206.

11 Quotation from page 305 of Carter, P. L. (2006). Straddling boundaries: Identity, culture, and school. *Sociology of Education, 79*(4), 304-328.

12 Quotation from page 20 of Ogbu, J. U. (2004). Collective identity and the burden of "acting White" in Black history, community, and education. *The Urban Review, 36*(1), 1-35.

13 Ogbu, J. U. (2004).

14 For example, see O'Connor, C. (1997). Dispositions toward

(collective) struggle and educational resilience in the inner city: A case analysis of six African-American high school students. *American Educational Research Journal, 34*(4), 593-629.

15 Horvat, E. M., and Lewis, K. S. (2003). Reassessing the "burden of 'acting White'": The importance of peer groups in managing academic success. *Sociology of Education, 76*(4), 265-280.

16 For example, see Pinder, P. J. (2013). Cultural, ethnic differences, parental involvement differences, and educational achievement of African heritage students: Towards employing a culturally sensitive curriculum in K–12 classrooms, a literature review. *Journal of African American Studies, 17*(2), 116-128.

17 Wiggan, G. (2007). Race, school achievement, and educational inequality: Toward a student-based inquiry perspective. *Review of Educational Research, 77*(3), 310-333.

18 Louie, V. (2007). Who makes the transition to college? Why we should care, what we know, and what we need to do. *The Teachers College Record, 109*(10), 2222-2251.

19 For example, see Nisbett, R. E., Peng, K., Choi, I., and Norenzayan, A. (2001).

20 Muramoto, Y., Yamaguchi, S., and Kim, U. (2009). Perception of achievement attribution in individual and group contexts: Comparative analysis of Japanese, Korean, and Asian-American results. *Asian Journal of Social Psychology,12*(3), 199-210.

21 For example, see Choi, I., Nisbett, R. E., and Norenzayan, A. (1999). Causal attribution across cultures: Variation and universality. *Psychological Bulletin, 125*(1), 47-63.

22 For an excellent review, see Steele, C. M. (1997). A threat in the air: How stereotypes shape intellectual identity and performance. *American Psychologist, 52*(6), 613-629.

23 Brown, R. P., and Lee, M. N. (2005). Stigma consciousness and the race gap in college academic achievement. *Self and Identity, 4*(2), 149-157.

24 Wiggan, G. (2007).

25 Markus, H. R., and Kitayama, S. (1991). Culture and the self: Implications for cognition, emotion, and motivation. *Psychological Review, 98*(2), 224-253.

26 Markus, H. R., and Kitayama, S. (1991).

27 Zusho, A., Pintrich, P. R., and Cortina, K. S. (2005). Motives, goals, and adaptive patterns of performance in Asian American and Anglo American students. *Learning and Individual differences, 15*(2), 141-

158.

28 This was consistent with Elliot, A. J., and Church, M. A. (1997). A hierarchical model of approach and avoidance achievement motivation. *Journal of Personality and Social Psychology,72*(1), 218-232.

29 Salili, F., and Lai, M. K. (2003). Learning and motivation of Chinese students in Hong Kong: A longitudinal study of contextual influences on students' achievement orientation and performance. *Psychology in the Schools*, *40*(1), 51-70.

30 Eaton, M. J., and Dembo, M. H. (1997). Differences in the motivational beliefs of Asian American and non-Asian students. *Journal of Educational Psychology, 89*(3), 433-440.

31 Yoshino, A. (2012). The relationship between self-concept and achievement in TIMSS 2007: A comparison between American and Japanese Students. *International Review of Education, 58*(2), 199-219.

32 Heine, S. J., Kitayama, S., Lehman, D. R., Takata, T., Ide, E., Leung, C., and Matsumoto, H. (2001). Divergent consequences of success and failure in Japan and North America: An investigation of self-improving motivations and malleable selves. *Journal of Personality and Social Psychology, 81*(4), 599–615.

33 Strayhorn, T. L. (2011). Bridging the pipeline: Increasing underrepresented students' preparation for college through a summer bridge program. *American Behavioral Scientist, 55*(2), 142-159.

34 Purdie, N., Hattie, J., and Douglas, G. (1996). Student conceptions of learning and their use of self-regulated learning strategies: A cross-cultural comparison. *Journal of Educational Psychology*, *88*(1), 87-100.

35 Quotation from pages 230-231 of Markus, H. R., and Kitayama, S. (1991).

36 Iyengar, S. S., and Lepper, M. R. (1999). Rethinking the value of choice: a cultural perspective on intrinsic motivation. *Journal of Personality and Social Psychology*, *76*(3), 349-366.

ABOUT THE AUTHOR – TROY DVORAK

I was born in Minnesota but I grew up in Canada. I lived in Canada for 26 years and completed all of my schooling there. In 1996 I graduated with a Master's degree in Psychology. For the first 7.5 years of my career, I worked as a psychometrist at a children's mental health agency, providing psychological assessment and treatment services to kids, teens, and families. In October 2003, I moved back to Minnesota and began teaching psychology classes at a few community colleges.

In my personal life I enjoy traveling and playing and listening to music. I am a self-taught drummer and just started trying to learn the guitar in 2014. I am a huge fan of 80s hard rock and "hair" metal. That's pretty much all I listen to. Yes, this college prof ROCKS!

Made in the USA
Middletown, DE
06 May 2015